REA

FRIENDS OF ACPL

D1067962

REA DO NOT REMOVE
CARDS FROM POCKET

923 .142 K53d   2198186
KIDD, CHARLES, 1952—
DEBRETT'S BOOK OF ROYAL
  CHILDREN /

ALLEN COUNTY PUBLIC LIBRARY

FORT WAYNE, INDIANA 46802

You may return this book to any agency, branch,
or bookmobile of the Allen County Public Library.

DEMCO

Debrett's Book of

Royal Children

The arms of the Prince and Princess of Wales.

Debrett's Book of

Royal Children

Charles Kidd & Patrick Montague-Smith

William Morrow and Company, Inc
New York 1982

Copyright © 1982 by Charles Kidd
and Patrick Montague-Smith

First published in Great Britain in 1982 by
Debrett's Peerage Ltd,
73/77 Britannia Road,
London SW6

First published in the United States of America
in 1982 by William Morrow and Company, Inc.

All rights reserved. No part of this book may be
reproduced or utilized in any form or by any means,
electronic or mechanical, including photocopying,
recording or by any information storage and retrieval
system, without permission in writing from the
Publisher. Inquiries should be addressed to William
Morrow and Company, Inc., 105 Madison Avenue,
New York, N.Y. 10016.

Library of Congress Catalog Card Number: 82-80677
ISBN: 0-688-01380-5

Edited, designed and produced by
Shuckburgh Reynolds Ltd,
8 Northumberland Place, London W2 5BS
on behalf of Debrett's Peerage Ltd

ALLEN COUNTY PUBLIC LIBRARY
FORT WAYNE, INDIANA

Design: Mel Petersen & Associates
Designer: Linda Abraham
Art Editor: Mel Petersen
Picture research: Linda Proud

Typesetting by SX Composing Ltd,
Rayleigh, Essex

Printed and bound in the Netherlands by L. Van Leer

First U.S. Edition
1 2 3 4 5 6 7 8 9 10

Contents

2136186

Introduction   6

Queen Victoria's Children   16

Edward VII's Children   42

George V's Children   68

George VI's Children   92

Elizabeth II's Children   112

The Royal Cousins   138

The Princess of Wales   160

The Royal Baby   172

Royal Ancestry   178

List of Books   200

Index   201

Acknowledgements   208

Introduction

The Queen and Prince Philip posed for a photograph on February 6th 1982, thirty years to the day after her accession to the throne. Behind is Sandringham House.

Franz Winterhalter's famous painting of Queen Victoria and her family, completed in 1847. The children, from left to right, are Prince Alfred, the Prince of Wales, Princess Alice, Princess Helena and the Princess Royal.

Although Britain's monarchy is one of the most ancient in the world, it has been astonishingly successful in adapting to the times and keeping in touch with the wishes and sentiments of the people. Sceptical commentators have often been astounded by the immense feelings of love, loyalty and popularity which the royal family remains able to evoke among the British people and even elsewhere in the Commonwealth. When the Queen celebrated her silver jubilee in 1977, most foreign observers were amazed by the way economic troubles and political strife were set aside that summer, and the whole population seemed to unite in its demonstrations of affection for her. Four years later, when her son took Lady Diana Spencer for his wife in St Paul's Cathedral, the acclamation they received almost outshone even that heady jubilee year. Now their first child is born, and we have another chance to see how close our royal family and its fortunes are to the hearts of millions of people.

The House of Windsor, inaugurated by King George V in 1917, now has five generations in the direct line. The Queen herself now has three grandchildren, the other two being Peter and Zara Phillips. She is the forty-first sovereign since the Norman conquest; and her eldest son is the twenty-first Prince of Wales. This extraordinary continuity is a vital ingredient in the success of the English monarchy, as even its detractors recognise. As John Grigg has said: "The Monarchy . . . emphasises the unity of the living with the living, of the living with the dead, and of the living with those as yet unborn." In other words, the monarchy focusses that sense of national unity and historical destiny which all mature societies seem to need; and Britain is by any standards a mature and stable society.

There are many other reasons for the success of the monarchy and the popularity of the royal family. With very few exceptions in the last 150 years, British kings and queens have shown remarkable sensitivity to the demands of new times. They have avoided political or sectarian partisanship. They have shown a highly developed sense of duty — almost like an inherited talent, which one can see passed down from Queen Victoria to Queen Elizabeth II and beyond. They have shown a fine sense of the balance between dignity and accessibility, adapting to changing

The Duchess of York with her second daughter Princess Margaret in 1932.

Princess Margaret in 1938 at the age of eight, a portrait photograph by Marcus Adams.

circumstances while holding on to the most valuable traditions.

One of the most obvious changes during the 140 years of monarchy covered by this book is the transition from the virtually unknown image of members of the royal family into the worldwide television and newspaper coverage we know today. Queen Victoria, although known by sight at home, and as "the great white Queen" to her empire, from her photographs, stamps and coinage, was almost as far removed from ordinary people as the deity. It was not until the age of the cinema newsreels that princes and princesses could readily be recognised by the vast majority.

The arrival of live-coverage filming coincided with the early childhood of George V's grandchildren, the young Princesses Elizabeth and Margaret Rose, whose activities were always spotlighted. Today every viewer knows far more than mere appearances; he has a personal identification with the "royals". This familiarity has resulted in their being called by their christian names rather than by titles. When the Duke of Windsor was Prince of Wales, no one called him Edward; yet today the Prince of Wales and the Duke of Edinburgh are almost universally known as "Charles" and "Philip", usually without a "prince". To millions of people only their own immediate family circle is more familiar to them than the royal family. This is no doubt one reason why royal popularity has been so much enhanced in recent generations.

But the strain imposed on individual members of the royal family by this relatively recent development is self-evident. On several occasions in the last few years they have become so harrassed by photographers and journalists that outbursts against the press have occurred. When Lady Diana Spencer emerged overnight from obscurity into the full blaze of public and press attention, she found the experience shattering although she stood it with great fortitude. Even after her engagement to the Prince of Wales was officially announced, the harrassment continued relentlessly; and eventually the Queen herself called a press conference, which she personally attended, to plead with editors to respect the privacy of the newest recruit to the royal ranks.

We follow throughout this book the birth, childhood and upbringing – and more briefly the later lives – of the children of our kings and queens from Victoria to the present day. Reviewing this story, one is struck by the remarkably consistent way in which the British royal family have upheld the best standards of their time over such things as methods of childbirth and attitudes to parenthood and the upbringing of children. Queen Victoria by her example made respectable the use of anaesthetics during labour. She was an unusually devoted mother to her young children, and took exceptional pains over their early education. Her descendants, right up to the present day, have been equally assiduous in their parental responsibilities, while moving with the times over matters of education and upbringing. When Prince Charles and Princess Anne were small children, for example, they were taught to bow and curtsey formally whenever they approached their great grandmother Queen Mary, for even in private a monarch's dignity was sacrosanct. The Queen and Prince Philip, however, dispensed with this slight barrier, so far as they were concerned, to natural family relationships.

Prince Charles and Princess Anne in the spring of 1954.

The kind of family life that royal children received has naturally varied in the five generations of parenthood. Queen Victoria and the Prince Consort were never happier than when they were away from rigid court ceremonial at Osborne and Balmoral, where they could indulge in homely activities, such as excursions and picnics. As Queen Regnant, Victoria was limited by her onerous duties until she went into voluntary "retirement" on Albert's death; but although a devoted mother she and Albert were unduly harsh in their treatment of their son and heir, the Prince of Wales, later Edward VII; and all their children were subjected to rigid discipline.

Lord Snowdon's photograph of Princess Anne with her first child, Peter, in the grounds of her home, Gatcombe Park, in 1978.

Queen Victoria's daughter-in-law Alexandra, when Princess of Wales, went to the other extreme. She smothered her children with maternal love and did not resort to any discipline to speak of. With her son and daughter-in-law, the future King George V and Queen Mary, on the other hand, there was an impenetrable barrier between them and their young children. According to Randolph Churchill, George V once told Lord Derby: "My father was frightened of his mother; I was frightened of my father; I'm damned well going to see to it that my children are frightened of me." Although this story may well be apocryphal, his children *were* frightened of him, and his wife little understood them in their early

The Queen and her family (far left) make frequent trips to Commonwealth nations. In 1976 they were in Canada for the Commonwealth Games.

Prince Philip and his young son Prince Edward (left) in 1968, looking for fish in the lake at Frogmore.

The Prince and Princess of Wales appear on the Buckingham Palace balcony after their wedding in July 1981.

The royal couple coming down the aisle of St Paul's Cathedral, followed by the chief bridesmaid Lady Sarah Armstrong-Jones.

In 1972 the Queen and her family (left) gathered at Windsor Castle to celebrate her Silver Wedding, and were photographed by Lord Lichfield. Standing, from the left, are Lord Snowdon, the Duke of Kent, Prince Michael, Prince Philip, Lord St Andrews, Prince Charles, Prince Andrew, Angus Ogilvy and his son James Ogilvy. Seated are Princess Margaret, the Duchess of Kent (holding Lord Nicholas Windsor), the Queen Mother, the Queen, Princess Anne, Marina Ogilvy and Princess Alexandra. On the floor are Lady Sarah Armstrong-Jones, Lord Linley, Prince Edward and Lady Helen Windsor.

The Queen with Prince Charles aged one; and (top) Princess Anne aged two.

years. The Duke and Duchess of York did not repeat this mistake, for both were devoted to their two daughters, the present Queen and Princess Margaret, who had a comparatively simple upbringing at 145, Piccadilly and the Royal Lodge, Windsor, until their father unexpectedly was called to the throne as King George VI on his elder brother's abdication. His daughters were then respectively aged nine and five years.

The Queen and Prince Philip have also given their children an extremely happy home life. Prince Charles and Princess Anne were still in the nursery at the ages of three and just under two when their mother succeeded to the throne, which meant moving from Clarence House to Buckingham Palace. Although the Queen's accession limited the time she could devote to her children, informality today has resulted in a much more relaxed court than in the time of her great great grandmother, Queen Victoria.

To some extent parenthood and parental attitudes have changed less than one might think in the last century and a half. The nine children of Queen Victoria were certainly dressed in a very much stiffer and more formal way than royal children are today, and they sometimes look sadly out from the early photographs reproduced here like little stuffed dolls. But one must remember that this was then the custom in the fashionable world; and there were the limitations of the fledgling art of photography in those days: the exposure time of several seconds meant that everyone had to sit or stand rigid and motionless while the photographer worked. The instant informal snapshot was still technically out of reach. But the children themselves were as lively, headstrong and individualist as their modern counterparts, and there are plenty of hilarious anecdotes to confirm this.

Prince Philip, like his predecessor as a queen's husband, Prince Albert, is master of his own house, and as such played a large part in determining the education of his children. But the results have been very different. Victoria's and Albert's offspring were shielded from the world outside by tutors and governesses, when the Prince of Wales yearned in vain for the companionship of other boys of his own age. The Queen and Prince Philip, instead of isolating their children, gave them the best possible education. Prince Charles was the first heir to the throne to have gone to school, mixing with other boys as equals.

Doubtless there will be those who will criticise the Prince and Princess of Wales if they decide to send their children to similar schools rather than take advantage of the state system. But those near to the throne should be given the type of education that would best train them for their future role. This may well prove to be boarding schools, where it would be much easier to safeguard children's privacy and to ensure adequate security.

Another matter on which attitudes and practices have changed over the last 150 years is the question of royal ceremonial. Queen Victoria was loath to part with any customs which upheld the dignity of the monarchy, and she had quite a taste for pomp and ceremonial. The christening ceremonies of all her nine children were staged with an immense panoply of grandeur: the Lancaster and Windsor heralds of arms led the procession into the private chapel at Windsor, followed in state by the godparents, foreign ambassadors, the Prime Minister and his cabinet colleagues, and Garter King of Arms. When her first child, Princess Victoria, was born Prince Albert himself designed a spectacular font for the christening, made of silver gilt, and decorated with water lilies and the royal arms. An exquisite christening robe was made from the finest Honiton lace. Both the font and the robe have been used for almost all royal christenings ever since, although the ceremonial surrounding the baptism is now more modest and in tune with the age.

It is sometimes said that the royal family could go much further in "democratising" the monarchy and abandoning "outdated" customs, as some European royal families have done. The Queen herself has shown that she has some sympathy with this view, and has made some important adjustments in the style of royal behaviour and the degree of public access to the royal family. For example, soon after her accession she instituted small informal luncheon parties of about eight guests from widely differing walks of life, held regularly at Buckingham Palace in preference to formal evening dinner parties. The old ceremonial "presentation at court" was replaced by the three annual garden parties, to each of which up to 8,000 guests may be invited. She has also become celebrated for her "walkabouts", an innovation first introduced in

Mabel Anderson (above), nanny to Prince Charles and Princess Anne. For a time she went on to look after Princess Anne's first child at Gatcombe Park.

Prince Charles went to Cheam preparatory school when he was eight. Here he is taking part in the school sports day.

Princess Anne and her husband Mark Phillips in 1981, when she was expecting her second child Zara.

The Duchess of Gloucester (opp. top left). She met the Duke when she was studying languages at Cambridge.

Princess Michael of Kent (opp. top right). Since she is a Catholic, Prince Michael forfeited his place in the line of succession.

The Princess of Wales has undertaken numerous public engagements since her marriage, and continues to captivate the hearts of the public with her beauty and high spirits.

New Zealand twelve years ago, as a means of speaking to people who may never be invited to a garden or luncheon party, but whose loyalty and support she nevertheless values and needs. A more recent innovation has been her Christmas television broadcasts, started on the radio by her grandfather George V in 1932, in which she appears informally with other members of her family. There have also been some very popular "behind the scenes" films showing the royal family at home. The Prince and Princess of Wales, Prince Philip, Princess Margaret and Princess Anne have all taken part in informal television and radio interviews, which twenty years ago would still have been unthinkable.

On the other hand, it is widely accepted that royal dignity and ceremonial have a very important part to play in the nation's life. They uphold the authority of the sovereign's place at the centre of the British Constitution, as the Head of State and of the established Church, as well as many other national institutions.

An important feature of the nation's life is the number of engagements carried out by the royal family. Fortunately today there are more members able to participate in these greatly valued occasions than at any time since the death of Queen Victoria in 1901. Despite their age, the Queen Mother and the Queen's aunt, Princess Alice, Duchess of Gloucester, still manage to perform many official duties.

The Queen and Prince Philip will have increasing help from the younger members of their family. The Prince and Princess of Wales, with more and more responsibilities as time goes on, have already been joined by Prince Andrew. Now that Prince Edward has reached adulthood, he too is beginning to participate. Other members of the royal family who assist are Princess Anne, Princess Margaret, the Dukes and Duchesses of Gloucester and Kent, Prince and Princess Michael, and Princess Alexandra.

As several of the younger generation have not inherited the title of H.R.H., they will be unable to help in the official programme. These are the children of Princess Anne, Princess Margaret, Princess Alexandra, the Dukes of Gloucester and Kent, and Prince Michael. In due course we can expect the important participation of the Prince and Princess of Wales's children, although it will not be until the next century that they will be old enough!

Queen Victoria's Children

"I think you will see with me the great
inconvenience a large family would
be to all of us, and particularly to the
country, independent of the hardship and
inconvenience to myself. Men never think,
at least seldom think, what a hard task it is
for us women to go through . . ."
– Queen Victoria

*Queen Victoria with her youngest
child, Princess Beatrice, who
married Prince Henry of
Battenberg. On the right is the
Queen's grand-daughter Princess
Louis of Battenberg (who
married Prince Henry's elder
brother), nursing her daughter
Princess Alice – who became
mother of Prince Philip.*

Prince Leopold aged six (far left). He is dressed as a son of Henry IV, from the last scene of Shakespeare's Richard II. He wore this costume at the bal costumé held at Buckingham Palace on 7 April 1859.

Bertie and Louise as "winter" (left) in the Tableaux of Seasons held at Windsor on 10 February 1854, photographed by Roger Fenton. Note the skates in the foreground.

Vicky and Arthur as "summer" (below).

Alice as "spring" (right).

Helena as "the spirit empress" (far right).

Arthur and Alfred in Sikh Indian dress, at Osborne on 6 September 1854 (below).

Bertie and Alfred with their tutor, Frederick Gibbs, February 1854, photographed by Roger Fenton.

Queen Victoria's second daughter, Princess Alice, and her husband Prince Louis of Hesse, with their children. He is carrying the youngest, May. The other children, from the left, are Ella, Ernest, Alix (later the Tsarina, murdered in 1918), Irene and Victoria (later Princess Louis of Battenberg). As was then the fashion, all the girls are dressed alike.

QUEEN VICTORIA'S CHILDREN

Queen Victoria sits at a table in the grounds at Osborne, with a family group ranged round her. To the left of her, standing, are her grandson the Duke of York (George V) with his son Prince Albert (George VI), and her grand-daughter Princess Margaret of Connaught (Crown Princess of Sweden). Seated are the Duchess of York (Queen Mary) with her children Princess Mary (Princess Royal) and Prince Edward (Duke of Windsor); Princess Aribert of Anhalt (Marie Louise); Prince Leopold of Battenberg; and (on the ground) Prince Alexander of Battenberg. Standing to the right of the Queen is her grandson Prince Arthur of Connaught, and seated are the Duchess of Connaught (nonchalantly reading a newspaper), Princess Henry of Battenberg (Princess Beatrice) and Princess Victoria of Schleswig-Holstein. In between, standing, are Princess Ena of Battenberg (Queen of Spain) and Prince Maurice of Battenberg. Princess Patricia of Connaught (Lady Patricia Ramsay), with her dog, is on the ground to the right. The year is 1897.

22

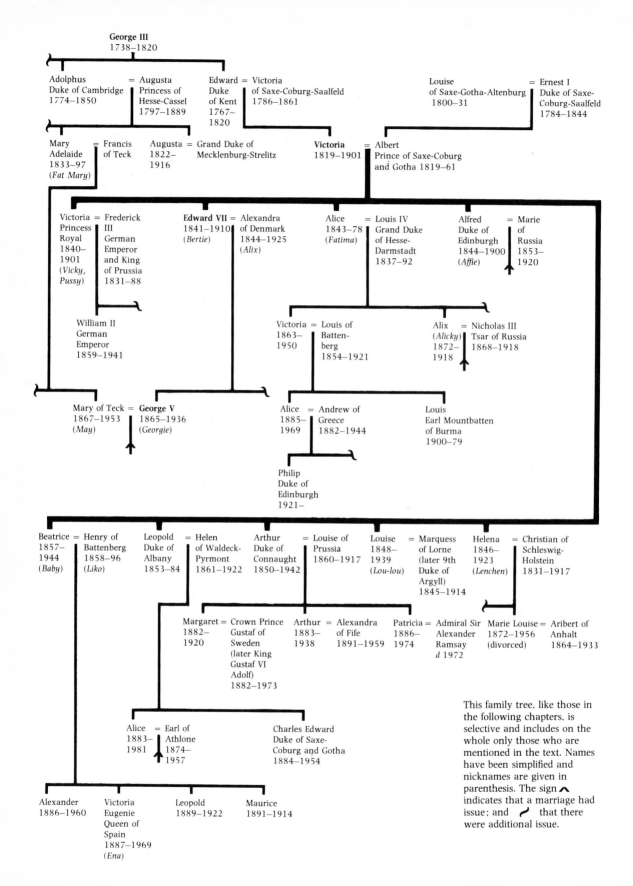

George III
1738–1820

Adolphus
Duke of Cambridge
1774–1850

= Augusta
Princess of
Hesse-Cassel
1797–1889

Edward = Victoria
Duke of Saxe-Coburg-Saalfeld
of Kent 1786–1861
1767–
1820

Louise
of Saxe-Gotha-Altenburg
1800–31

= Ernest I
Duke of Saxe-
Coburg-Saalfeld
1784–1844

Mary
Adelaide
1833–97
(Fat Mary)

= Francis
of Teck

Augusta = Grand Duke of
1822– Mecklenburg-Strelitz
1916

Victoria
1819–1901

= Albert
Prince of Saxe-Coburg
and Gotha 1819–61

Victoria = Frederick
Princess III
Royal German
1840– Emperor
1901 and King
(Vicky, of Prussia
Pussy) 1831–88

Edward VII = Alexandra
1841–1910 of Denmark
(Bertie) 1844–1925
(Alix)

Alice = Louis IV
1843–78 Grand Duke
(Fatima) of Hesse-
Darmstadt
1837–92

Alfred = Marie
Duke of of
Edinburgh Russia
1844–1900 1853–
(Affie) 1920

William II
German
Emperor
1859–1941

Victoria = Louis of
1863– Batten-
1950 berg
1854–1921

Alix = Nicholas III
(Alicky) Tsar of Russia
1872– 1868–1918
1918

Mary of Teck = George V
1867–1953 1865–1936
(May) (Georgie)

Alice = Andrew of
1885– Greece
1969 1882–1944

Louis
Earl Mountbatten
of Burma
1900–79

Philip
Duke of
Edinburgh
1921–

Beatrice = Henry of
1857– Battenberg
1944 1858–96
(Baby) (Liko)

Leopold = Helen
Duke of of Waldeck-
Albany Pyrmont
1853–84 1861–1922

Arthur = Louise of
Duke of Prussia
Connaught 1860–1917
1850–1942

Louise = Marquess
1848– of Lorne
1939 (later 9th
(Lou-lou) Duke of
Argyll)
1845–1914

Helena = Christian of
1846– Schleswig-
1923 Holstein
(Lenchen) 1831–1917

Margaret = Crown Prince
1882– Gustaf of
1920 Sweden
(later King
Gustaf VI
Adolf)
1882–1973

Arthur = Alexandra
1883– of Fife
1938 1891–1959

Patricia = Admiral Sir
1886– Alexander
1974 Ramsay
d 1972

Marie Louise = Aribert of
1872–1956 Anhalt
(divorced) 1864–1933

Alice = Earl of
1883– Athlone
1981 1874–
1957

Charles Edward
Duke of Saxe-
Coburg and Gotha
1884–1954

This family tree, like those in
the following chapters, is
selective and includes on the
whole only those who are
mentioned in the text. Names
have been simplified and
nicknames are given in
parenthesis. The sign ⌃
indicates that a marriage had
issue; and ↰ that there
were additional issue.

Alexander
1886–1960

Victoria
Eugenie
Queen of
Spain
1887–1969
(Ena)

Leopold
1889–1922

Maurice
1891–1914

At the Chapel Royal, St James's Palace, on 10 February 1840, Queen Victoria married her first cousin, Prince Albert of Saxe-Coburg and Gotha. This was less than two and a half years after the eighteen-year-old Princess had been roused from her sleep at Kensington Palace to be told that her uncle, William IV, was no more and that she was Queen.

Prince Albert was considered to be the best looking of the eligible young men in Europe, but when his name was mentioned as a possible suitor, the young Queen said that she might like him "as a friend, and as a *cousin*, and as a *brother*, but not *more*". But when they met she confided in her diary that he had "such beautiful blue eyes, an exquisite nose and such a pretty mouth . . . a beautiful figure, broad in the shoulders and fine waist; my heart is quite going. . . ."

The match proved an ideal one for them both, even if life did not always go smoothly. Victoria was lucky that Albert never showed the slightest interest in other women, although she herself could occasionally show signs of jealousy. For instance it was said that Prince Albert once admired a bouquet carried by Miss Pitt, a maid of honour, and while he was examining it the Queen entered. After praising the flowers, she asked from where they came. "The presence of Miss Pitt was dispensed with", we are told. "Victoria seized the bouquet, and scattered its fragments over the room."

The chief cause of dissention between them was the intractable Baroness Lehzen, the Queen's former governess and now her attendant — "that most dear being", the Queen had called her. She had exercised a powerful influence over Victoria since her childhood, and went on to dominate the royal household. Prince Albert found the Queen's dependence on her worrying, and he suspected her evil influence in every domestic difficulty. He was driven to call her "a crazy, common, stupid intriguer, obsessed with lust of power, who regards herself as a demi-god, and anyone who refused to acknowledge her as such, as a criminal". Eventually he won the day, and the Baroness was sent home to Germany.

Charles Greville, the diarist, wrote of the royal couple's walk on the first morning of their honeymoon, that it was "strange that a bridal night should be so short; and I told Lady Palmerston that this was not the way to provide us with a Prince of Wales".

The wedding of Queen Victoria to Prince Albert in 1840, as recorded by Sir George Hayter. This is a contemporary engraving from his painting.

Greville was proved wrong. For although the Queen had already said that having children was "the *only* thing I *dread*", by the end of March she was complaining of feeling unwell, and instead of gallops and waltzes at court balls, she went back to more stately quadrilles. There was no announcement, but "the knowing Ladies are all confident she is with child", wrote one peer.

On the evening of 10 June, as the Queen and Prince set out for a drive from Buckingham Palace in her open phaeton, a shot was fired in Constitution Hill only six paces away. The horses reared and the carriage stopped. The assailant, who proved to be a 17-year-old waiter from an inn, was seen brandishing two pistols, when he fired a second shot. The Prince later wrote, "my chief anxiety was lest the fright should prove injurious to Victoria in her present state, but she is quite well". Everyone thought of Princess Charlotte, the Prince Regent's only child and direct heir to the throne, who had died in childbirth 23 years earlier. A Regency Bill was hurried through Parliament by Lord Melbourne, the Prime Minister, appointing Albert as the Regent in the event of the Queen's death leaving an infant to succeed her.

A Canon of St George's Chapel, Windsor, suggested to the Prince that a special prayer should be offered for the Queen. "No! No!" he was told, "you have one already in the litany – all women labouring of child, and you pray three times for the Queen." Still unconvinced, the Canon asked, "Sir, can one pray too much for Her Majesty?" "Not too *heartily*," agreed Albert, "but too *often*."

On the night of 21 November, the Queen woke up at Buckingham Palace feeling very uncomfortable, although the child was not expected for over a fortnight. She roused Albert "with difficulty", and he fetched the doctor, Sir James Clark who, in turn, sent for the obstetrician, Dr Locock. So unexpected was it that the wet nurse was still at home in the Isle of Wight. She had to be fetched by a page and brought in an open boat, arriving at the Palace by two in the morning. "Nothing ready," observed Greville. At about 2 pm on the following day, a daughter was born, to be named Victoria after her mother, but known to her parents as Pussy, Pussette, or Vicky. She was immediately styled the Princess Royal, the title reserved for a Sovereign's eldest daughter for life.

As the Queen objected to a large number of people being present

The historic lily font, first made for the christening of the Princess Royal in 1841. It was designed by her father the Prince Consort, and has been used at nearly every royal christening ever since.

round her, only the Prince, the doctor, and the monthly nurse, Mrs Lilly, were in the room at the time. The rest, including the Archbishop of Canterbury, the Bishop of London, the Lord Steward of the Household, and other dignitaries, waited in the adjoining room with the door open. The naked child was carried for their inspection and placed on a table.

When the baby was delivered, Dr Locock said, "Oh, Madam, it is a Princess", to which the Queen breezily answered, "Never mind, the next will be a Prince". She thought the country would be disappointed in the birth of a girl, but here she was wrong. Any life between her and the heir presumptive, her detested uncle Ernest, King of Hanover, was splendid news. It was popularly thought that he had designs on the English throne, and many people remembered how he had once proposed a toast to the heir when at

The christening of the Princess Royal in the Throne Room at Buckingham Palace on 10 February 1841, from a drawing by C. R. Leslie in Windsor Castle. The Queen and Prince Consort are on the right.

Windsor with his brother, William IV, with the proviso "God bless him", to which William angrily corrected, "God bless her". It had also been noted that the would-be assassin in Constitution Hill had carried pistols which were silver mounted with the monogram "ER". Victoria later discounted this theory about her wicked uncle; and as for having a girl first, she was pleased, "as they were less trouble than boys".

Queen Victoria did not believe in breast-feeding her own children, and when in later years she discovered that Alice was suckling hers, and once when she was ill Vicky was doing so in her place, she was horrified. That one of the royal cows was given the name Alice soon afterwards may not have been a mere coincidence.

The Queen recovered so rapidly that the court could travel to Windsor for Christmas. She and the Prince were back in London to celebrate not only their first wedding anniversary on 10 February 1841 but also their daughter's christening at the Chapel Royal, St James's. The silver gilt font, decorated with the Royal Arms, was designed by Prince Albert. This and the christening robe, made of Honiton lace, have since been used at subsequent Royal christenings. The cake had a sugar Britannia on top, carrying a miniature pink sugar Princess Royal.

Vicky was described at the age of eight months as "a fine, fat fair, royal-looking baby, too absurdly like the Queen". Victoria herself commented that "we find Pussy amazingly advanced in intelligence and also in naughtiness". A couple of years later the Princess told her governess, "I'm sorry I was naughty, but I mean to be just as naughty next time".

By the age of three, the young Princess could converse in English, German and French; and by four her admiring father was already thinking of her destiny. The heir to the King of Prussia, who was then invited to England for the christening of her brother Alfred, had a son of twelve, a potential bridegroom for the Princess Royal.

In the meantime, some months after Vicky's birth, the approaching second pregnancy was the subject of considerable speculation. One newspaper devoted the top of a column to the subject every week with the heading "THE LADIES *Pray remember/ The tenth of November*", and gave news of various ladies at court in a similar condition.

Victoria wrote to her uncle Leopold, King of the Belgians, in answer to his wish that Pussy would only be the first of her babies:

> I think, dearest Uncle, you cannot *really* wish me to be the mamma d'une *nombreuse* famille, for I think you will see with me the great inconvenience a large family would be to all of us, and particularly to the country, independent of the hardship and inconvenience to myself. Men never think, at least seldom think, what a hard task it is for us women to go through this *very often*.

Franz Winterhalter's portrait of Albert Edward, Prince of Wales, at the age of seven.

The second pregnancy was not easy. The Queen felt "wretched", and she was also anxious about Vicky who, unable to digest her food, had lost weight. "It is a great grief to see her so thin, pale and changed," she wrote. There was a violent scene between her and Prince Albert, which culminated in Lehzen's departure.

After a difficult confinement, early on 9 November 1841 the Queen gave birth to a son and heir, Albert Edward, known as Bertie. He was "a fine large boy", and only Pussy was "not at all pleased". This was the first male heir to the throne to be born almost within living memory. The last occasion was 79 years earlier with the birth of the future George IV.

Punch magazine, then five months old, celebrated the occasion with a long poem, which began:

> Huzza! We've a little Prince at last.
> A roaring Royal boy;
> And all day long the booming bells
> Have rung their peals of joy.

Rejoicings spread throughout the land and empire, and the Lord Chamberlain arranged an extra school holiday "by command of the Queen".

The heir to the throne was born Duke of Cornwall and Rothesay, and had a string of other titles, but he did not have to wait long for the most resonant title of all, which has to be specially created. Letters patent were issued on 4 December for the new Prince of Wales. Following his christening in St George's Chapel, Windsor, a banquet was given in the State Dining Room, where an enormous punchbowl, designed by George IV, was filled with 30 dozen bottles of mulled claret for toasts to the new Prince. Later that evening, at a reception in the Waterloo Chamber, the eight-foot round christening cake was cut and distributed.

One of the guests, little known to the general public, was the German, Baron Stockmar, one time mentor of Uncle Leopold, who despatched him to serve the Queen soon after her accession. He was forever lecturing the Queen on subjects of morality and duty, and even Lord Melbourne complained that "this damned morality will ruin everything". Wherever Victoria and Albert went Stockmar followed, except for four months in the year when he joined his wife and family in Coburg.

The running of the royal nursery was proving difficult. There was some criticism of Mrs Southey, the poet's sister-in-law, who had been recommended as governess by the Archbishop of Canterbury. In March 1842 she was pressed to resign when a successor could be found, and this appointment was given to Lady Lyttelton, a widow, who was one of the Queen's ladies. Both the Queen and Lord Melbourne agreed that a governess of high rank would have greater authority. Not only was she highly intelligent, but the Queen liked her, even if she disapproved of her high church views. Lady Lyttelton, whom the children called "Laddle", was born Lady Sarah Spencer and belonged to the same family as the present Princess of Wales.

With her third pregnancy, the Queen went over the baby linen with Lady Lyttelton, and was delighted to find that almost nothing new would be required. Princess Alice was born on 25 April 1843. Her father nicknamed her Fatima, considering this plump little baby would be the family beauty. When the Queen was out of the nursery, he prepared a surprise for her next birthday in May, by smuggling in the animal painter Edwin Landseer to paint the Princess in her cradle, with Dandie, a terrier to guard her. Albert presented the resulting portrait, which he surrounded with flowers, to the delighted Queen.

Lady Lyttelton found the Princess Royal, whom she called "Princessy", over-sensitive and inclined to be temperamental and occasionally untruthful. Once Vicky assured her French governess, Mlle Charrier, that Laddle (Lady Lyttelton) had given her permission to drop the Mademoiselle, which was not so. Then, in 1845, she claimed that Lady Lyttelton had desired her to wear her pink bonnet, although the subject had not been raised. Vicky was given to fits of rage and shrieking, for which "forcible arguments" had to be used. These turned out successfully, and their relations remained cordial.

Princess Alice, too, had attacks of sudden rage, and was given to flinging herself down and beating her head on the floor. When she was aged four, Laddle had to whip her for not telling the truth. The governess considered that as the case was very grave, she should obey "his Highness's instructions best" by administering a real punishment.

The surprise painting by Edwin Landseer of Princess Alice in her cradle, with Dandie the terrier to guard her.

*Prince Alfred's christening in the
private chapel at Windsor Castle,
14 September 1844.*

*Queen Victoria's second son,
Alfred, playing the violin. This
very early photograph, dated
8 February 1854, was taken by
the pioneer photographer
Roger Fenton.*

Windsor Castle was the birthplace of Prince Alfred, known to the royal family as Affie, on 6 August 1844 – the only one of the children not to have been born at Buckingham Palace. At the age of eighteen months he showed "a very good manly temper", which he retained for the rest of his life.

A few years later, when the Queen was driving through the streets with Bertie opposite her and Affie next to her, Bertie behaved impeccably, waving his hat and smiling to the crowd. Affie, on the other hand, looked sulky, with his hat firmly on his head and glaring in front of him. The Queen, bowing and smiling to left and right, appeared not to watch her sons. Then suddenly, without stopping her bows, she managed to knock off Affie's hat with one hand, and to give him a resounding clout on the side of his face with the other.

Bertie and his high-spirited sister, Vicky, were not always well behaved. "The children had a tremendous fight in our room," wrote their mother, "which really is too absurd." Mrs Lilly, the nurse, also told of the housemaid who, about to be married, had spread her bridal gown across her bed. Bertie crept into her room and smeared it all over with black lead. The result was a horse-whipping by Prince Albert. Although an affectionate boy, he continually suffered from comparison with his unusually bright elder sister. Baron Stockmar, whose attitude was "if he does not like books, he must be made to like them", continually prejudiced his parents against him. Prince Albert, though he enjoyed romping with his children in the nursery, was a martinet where education was concerned, and he and the Queen constantly let the boy know how backward he was.

A close bond of friendship grew up between Alice and Bertie. She always managed to bring out the best in him, but again comparisons were made. The Queen noted that when Bertie was aged six he had only advanced as far as Alice, who was more than eighteen months his junior, and who as Lady Lyttelton had pointed out was "neither as studious nor so clever as the Princess Royal".

Following the birth of the fifth child, Helena, called Lenchen, on 25 May 1846, Queen Victoria, with the help of her husband and Baron Stockmar, formulated a detailed memorandum for the education and character training of their children. This was issued in January, and divided the children into three classes. The first comprised the children in the nursery to about the age of five. Apart from the baby, the royal children now comprised the Princess Royal aged six, the Prince of Wales, five, Princess Alice, three, and Prince Alfred, two.

The eldest children would move into class two in the following month. Sarah Hildyard, daughter of a Lincolnshire vicar, was selected as governess at a salary of £200, and she, with a German and a Swiss governess, would function under the direction of Lady Lyttelton. The Queen considered that Bertie should soon be given entirely over to tutors, "and taken away from the women". This third stage would start in April 1849.

Frederick Gibbs, the tutor whom Stockmar approved of but the boys disliked.

Accordingly, a pleasant assistant master at Eton, Henry Birch, was engaged as tutor. Prince Albert personally drew up the first timetable for a six-hour day, covering nine subjects, with every minute of the day accounted for. Stockmar soon decided that Birch was too easy going, and persuaded the Queen and Prince Albert that he was the wrong man for the job. Bertie did not improve, and the tutor was dismissed at the beginning of 1852. Lady Canning, a lady in waiting, recalled that "it has been a trouble and a sorrow to the Prince of Wales, who has done no end of touching things since he heard that he was to lose him three weeks ago. He is such an affectionate dear little fellow". Bertie, then aged ten, was put in the charge of a humourless intellectual named Frederick Gibbs, whom he grew greatly to dislike, but as Stockmar approved of him he was to last eight years.

By the time that Princess Louise was born on 18 March 1848, Europe was in a turmoil, and there were riots and unrest in London streets. The Queen, noting the unsettled state, thought that Louise, or Lou-lou as she was called, would turn out "something peculiar", but she was to prove the most artistic of her daughters. There was consternation at her christening in Buckingham Palace. The Queen's aged Aunt Gloucester lost track of the occasion. In the middle of the ceremony, she suddenly got up from her place and knelt at the Queen's feet. "Imagine our horror!" wrote Queen Victoria.

Helena and Louise, the two middle daughters, were to turn out very differently. Helena, though a tomboy, was plain and obedient, whereas Louise was pretty, although always something of a rebel. As often happens, they were never regarded with the same affection as their elder and younger sisters.

The next Prince, Arthur, was born on 1 May 1850, the great Duke of Wellington's 81st birthday, and accordingly the Duke was asked to become a godfather to his namesake. This pleased him, he said, more than all his decorations. On Prince Arthur's first birthday, which was also the opening of Prince Albert's Great Exhibition, Winterhalter recaptured the scene in his famous picture "The First of May 1851", showing the Duke presenting a golden casket to his godson, who was held in the Queen's arms. Behind stands Albert, holding a plan of the Great Exhibition. On Waterloo Day 1852 the little boy was taken to see his godfather at Apsley House, but by the following September, the Iron Duke was dead.

As befitted Wellington's godson, Prince Arthur from his earliest childhood enjoyed everything martial. He liked nothing better for a present than a gun or a sword. After an encounter with some stable cats while rescuing his terrier, he emerged scratched and bloody. His anxious governess asked what had happened. "Wounded," said Arthur, "in execution of my duty." Arthur was to become the Queen's favourite son, and the only one who caused her no trouble.

Prince Arthur at the age of seven, an early photographic study by Caldesi (1857).

In 1851, Lady Lyttelton had to leave the royal household to look after her motherless grandchildren, and another of the Queen's ladies, the widowed Lady Caroline Barrington, an elderly lady whose father Lord Grey had been once Prime Minister, took charge of the nursery. She remained in office until her death in 1875, when the Queen's youngest child had reached the age of eighteen. The nurses included Mrs Packer, née Augusta Gow, from Scotland, Mrs Ratsey who used to annoy Prince Albert by constantly teasing her charges with "boo-boo", Mrs Hull, who was known as "Old May" and Mrs Thurston, whose twenty years' service started in 1845, and continued with a lifetime of friendship with Princess Beatrice. After her retirement, the Princess provided her with a little house near Kensington Palace.

When the Queen's and Prince Albert's wedding anniversary came round in February 1853, she prayed for the safety of "our 7 children, & 8th . . . to appear in 2 months!" On this occasion, for the first time, the Queen was given chloroform during the course of her labour, and commented afterwards that "the effect was soothing, quieting & delightful beyond measure". The use of an anaesthetic during childbirth was still a novelty at this time, and there was intense controversy about it with the Book of Genesis being cited on both sides. Its opponents even argued that the sufferings of a mother during labour were nature's method of ensuring her love for the baby. Queen Victoria's use of anaesthetics, her refusal to accept that the pain of childbirth was a mother's

Queen Victoria holding her third son Arthur, the infant Duke of Connaught, to whom his godfather, the Duke of Wellington, presents a casket on his first birthday in 1851. Behind stands the Prince Consort. The painting by Franz Winterhalter is in the Royal collection. Arthur grew up to become the Queen's favourite son.

Prince Leopold playing table croquet at the Villa Liader, Cannes, on 7 February 1862.

inevitable burden, was one of her great gifts to her people.

The new prince, born on 7 April 1853, was named Leopold. He was immediately described as "very delicate". The parents were aghast when haemophilia was diagnosed. This dreaded bleeding disease, by which a minor accident could prove fatal, can only occur in a male and is carried by a female (or through the genes of an affected male). Leopold was segregated from the boistrous games of his brothers and sisters, and the Queen became passionately concerned to protect him from accidents. Yet she could still give her usual frank opinion about her fourth and youngest son. When he was aged four she wrote, "he is tall, but holds himself worse than ever, and is a very common looking child, very plain in face, clever but an oddity — and not an engaging child, though amusing".

In 1854 the Queen made over to her children the delightful Swiss Cottage which had been brought over in sections to Osborne, Isle of Wight, and erected in the grounds near the sea. Here the boys learned carpentry and gardening, and the girls housekeeping and cookery. When their parents came, the princesses made cakes for tea parties, and the boys presented their garden produce. Each had his own plot of ground, and each tool and wheelbarrow was marked by the owner's initials. Behind the cottage is the miniature fort, built in 1860 by Prince Arthur. All these buildings may be seen today.

Though Dr Clark had warned the Prince Consort that the Queen "felt sure that if she had another child she would sink under it", a daughter, Beatrice, was born, very overdue, on 14 April 1857. On the contrary, despite a period of great tension, Victoria noted in her journal: "I have felt better and stronger this time than I have ever done before. . . . I was amply rewarded and forgot all I had gone through when I heard dearest Albert say 'it is a fine child, and a girl'."

By the time that Beatrice, her ninth and youngest child was born, the eldest, the Princess Royal, was already unofficially engaged to Fritz, Prince Frederick William of Prussia. The announcement was made in May, and one of the first duties of the couple was to stand as sponsors at Princess Beatrice's christening on 16 June. A few months later their wedding took place at St

*The Swiss Cottage at Osborne,
Isle of Wight, in 1897.*

James's, the bride being only two months over her 17th birthday. After the wedding, Vicky spent nearly all her spare time in England playing in the nursery with her baby sister.

Queen Victoria's letters to her eldest daughter in Prussia were full of news about "Baby". "Beatrice is now sitting in your little old chair, tapping on the table where her eight brothers and sisters played before her." At the age of two she could "jabber so fast and plain and is full of wit and fun and graceful as a fairy, meddles with everything, makes her remarks on all, quite exquisite". Albert, now officially the Prince Consort, sadly missed his favourite eldest daughter, and his main consolation was little Beatrice.

When Queen Victoria's world fell in, on her husband's death in 1861, Princess Beatrice had reached the age of four. To begin with, Princess Alice bore the brunt of her overwhelming grief. Everything at Osborne was kept as it had been during his life: the bed made every day and hot shaving water brought every morning. But Princess Alice escaped in the following year to marry Prince Louis of Hesse (a wedding which in the circumstances felt more like a funeral). From these early years as a small child, Princess Beatrice began her long training to be the Queen's constant companion. "Beatrice was the only thing I feel keeps me alive," Victoria wrote, but this child grew into a lonely, sad and repressed young woman, hardly ever apart from her mother.

*Prince Arthur, and his tutor
Major Elphinstone, photographed
by Prince Alfred in 1864 (when
he was twenty).*

Shortly after the Prince Consort's death, Queen Victoria wrote a memorandum of their life in minute detail. Both were awakened at 7 am by the wardrobe maid. Almost always Albert then got up and went to his sitting room to answer letters, prepare drafts, write his diary and read. "Formerly he used to be ready frequently before me. . . . If he was not ready, Baby [Princess Beatrice] generally went into his dressing room . . . and stopped with him till he followed with her. . . . At breakfast & luncheon & also our family dinners he sat at the top of the table & kept us all enlivened by his interesting conversation. . . . One of the children, or a visitor like Feodora [the Queen's half-sister] . . . sat between me and him & one of the younger children whom he constantly kept in order if they ate badly or untidily. . . . He could *not* bear bad manners & always dealt out his dear reprimands at the juveniles & a word from him was instantly obeyed."

In the winter Albert played ice hockey and the children skated, and when the Queen and he returned by train from Windsor to London they frequently took their two eldest and the youngest child with them as a treat.

Queen Victoria became known as the Grandmother of Europe due to the many dynastic marriages of her family. The King of Prussia became the German Emperor in 1871, but the Princess Royal's husband did not succeed him as Emperor Frederick III until 1888, when he was already suffering from cancer of the throat. During his brief reign of 99 days he was already incapable of speech. The widowed Empress Frederick, "die Engländerin", was long estranged from her bombastic son, Kaiser William II. The unhappy dowager Empress was taken seriously ill in 1901, a month after the death of her mother, Queen Victoria, whom she only survived by seven months.

Her eldest brother Bertie, Prince of Wales, after a long life of pleasure, succeeded his mother as King Edward VII. The three younger brothers, Alfred, Arthur and Leopold all received dukedoms, respectively of Edinburgh, Connaught and Albany. Prince Alfred served in the Royal Navy and married the Russian Grand Duchess Marie, Tsar Alexander II's only daughter, an autocratic princess who resented playing second fiddle to her beautiful sister-

A family group in April 1870. Queen Victoria is talking to the Princess of Wales, Alix, who holds her three-year-old daughter, Louise. The others, from the left, are the Queen's three youngest children, Beatrice (then 13), Leopold and Louise, and Alix's two boys Albert Victor and George.

in-law from Denmark. In 1893 her husband succeeded as the reigning Duke of Saxe-Coburg and Gotha on the death of his uncle Ernest, the Prince Consort's rakish brother. Neither the Duke, who died in 1900, nor the Duchess, became popular and many stories circulated about his drinking and bad temper.

Prince Arthur, Duke of Connaught, on the other hand, was a model member of the Royal Family. He fulfilled his childhood ambition by becoming a soldier and he long outlived his pleasant wife, Princess Louise of Prussia, and all his brothers and sisters except the youngest, when he died at the great age of 91 in January 1942.

The youngest and most studious of Queen Victoria's sons, Prince Leopold, Duke of Albany, acted as his mother's assistant for some years. She continually tried to curtail his activities due to his ill health, and remained extremely fond of him, despite his aversion to Balmoral. Nearly two years before his death in 1884, a few weeks before his 31st birthday, he made a happy marriage with Princess Helen of Waldeck, and left a daughter Alice, and posthumous son, Charles Edward. As a boy at Eton, Prince Charles Edward succeeded his uncle Alfred as the Duke of Saxe-Coburg

*The new-born Princess Victoria
of Hesse (above) with her nurse
Mrs Clarke, at Windsor in 1863.
She is Prince Philip's
grandmother.*

*Helen, Duchess of Albany, with
her children, nephews and niece
playing with their rocking horse
in April 1890. Her daughter
Princess Alice, in the saddle,
holds the baby Prince Leopold of
Battenberg, and her son Prince
Charles Edward is in the centre.
To the left is Prince Alexander
and to the right Princess Ena
(later Queen of Spain).*

*Queen Victoria holding her great
grandson Willy (above right),
later Kaiser Wilhelm II of
Germany.*

and Gotha, and later had the sadness of being on the opposite side
to Britain in World War I.

Princess Alice of Albany, aged only 13 months at her father's
death, married Queen Mary's brother, the Earl of Athlone. When
she died on 3 January 1981, not only was she the last of Queen
Victoria's 37 grandchildren, but at the age of 97 she was the oldest
member of the British Royal Family of all time.

Queen Victoria's second daughter, Princess Alice, who became
Grand Duchess of Hesse and the Rhine, had strong views on the
emancipation of women and a life-long interest in nursing and
education. She had practical nursing experience, and nursed her
own children, one of whom died, through an epidemic of diptheria.
She caught the infection herself, perhaps by kissing her suffering
little boy, and died on 14 December 1878 aged 35. By strange
coincidence this was the date of her father's tragic death in 1861;
and ten years later on the same day her brother Bertie all but died
of the same disease as his father, typhoid.

Queen Victoria took a great interest in Princess Alice's motherless children. These included Alix, last Tsarina of Russia, and
Victoria, who married Prince Louis of Battenberg, by whom she was
mother of Lord Mountbatten and grandmother of Prince Philip.

In 1866 Princess Helena, then aged 20, married a landless
German prince, fifteen years her senior, Prince Christian of Schleswig-Holstein, who became a naturalized British subject. This was
not without some spirited opposition from the Prince and Princess
of Wales (Christian had supported the Prussian side against

Denmark), and from the Princess Royal and Princess Alice, who thought their sister was being sacrificed at their mother's convenience. Later Lenchen's brother and sisters withdrew their objections when they realized that she was willing to seize this opportunity, rather than remain at her mother's beck and call, perhaps for the rest of her life. Their daughter, the gifted Princess Marie Louise, who died in 1956, thought up and brought to fruition Queen Mary's Doll's House, which can be seen today at Windsor Castle.

Princess Louise married in 1871 the Marquess of Lorne, later 9th Duke of Argyll, the first non-royal marriage of a Sovereign's daughter since Henry VIII's sister married Charles Brandon; but it was one which proved to be unhappy, and they later parted. An example of her work as a talented sculptress is the statue of her mother in Kensington Gardens, which the Queen unveiled at her Diamond Jubilee. She was the only one of Queen Victoria's offspring to have no children of her own. Like her brother, the Duke of Connaught, she lived to the age of 91, dying in December 1939.

The youngest of Queen Victoria's family, Princess Beatrice, had the most closeted upbringing of them all and, like them, was never allowed to be in a room with a man, even a brother, unaccompanied. In 1884, when attending the wedding at Darmstadt of her niece Victoria of Hesse to Louis of Battenberg, she fell in love with another guest, his younger brother, Prince Henry, who was called Liko.

When she told her mother the news, all relations between them were cut, except notes of the day's arrangements pushed over the breakfast table. For the second half of 1884 there is only one brief mention of Beatrice, and that in a postscript, in the Queen's *Journal and Letters*. However, eight months after their meeting, at Christmas, Prince Louis was able to persuade the Queen to accept his brother, but at a price. Beatrice and Liko had to remain with the Queen for her lifetime. Their wedding took place on 23 July 1885 in the little church of Whippingham near Osborne. Prince Henry joined the Ashanti Expedition in 1895, but contracted malaria, and died in January of the following year. Princess Beatrice remained with her mother to her death. She lived on until October 1944, and was buried at Whippingham. With her, Queen Victoria's family came to an end.

Princess Louise's sculpture of her mother outside Kensington Palace, which the Queen unveiled at her Diamond Jubilee of 1897.

Vicky's three older children, Prince William (Kaiser Wilhelm), Prince Henry and Princess Charlotte of Prussia, in July 1866.

Edward VII's Children

"If children are too strictly or perhaps
too severely treated they get shy and only
fear those whom they ought to love."
– Edward VII

*The Prince and Princess of
Wales with their two sons,
Albert Victor (on the right) and
George (later George V), in
1867.*

Prince George of Wales aged four; and, opposite, May of Teck, whom he eventually married, at much the same age.

44

A royal group photographed in a studio-prop train in August 1882. From the left are Princess Maud of Wales (Queen of Norway), King George I of Greece, his sister the Princess of Wales (Queen Alexandra), Princess Marie of Greece, Queen Louise of Denmark, Queen Olga of Greece, Princess Victoria of Wales, Princess Alexandra of Greece, Crown Prince Constantine of Greece, Princess Louise of Wales (Duchess of Fife), Prince George of Wales (George V), Prince George of Greece, and Prince Albert Victor of Wales (Duke of Clarence).

48

Queen Alexandra with her grandchildren, at Mar Lodge in 1904. She is holding Prince George of Wales (Duke of Kent). The others, from the left, are Prince Henry (Duke of Gloucester), Princess Alexandra of Fife, Prince Albert (George VI), Princess Maud of Fife, Prince Edward (Duke of Windsor) and Princess Mary (Princess Royal).

Alix holding her eldest grandson Prince Edward in 1897.

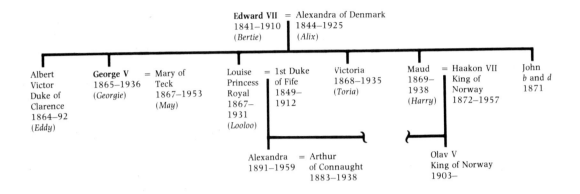

Edward VII = Alexandra of Denmark
1841–1910 | 1844–1925
(Bertie) (Alix)

Albert Victor Duke of Clarence 1864–92 (Eddy)

George V 1865–1936 (Georgie) = Mary of Teck 1867–1953 (May)

Louise Princess Royal 1867–1931 (Looloo) = 1st Duke of Fife 1849–1912

Victoria 1868–1935 (Toria)

Maud 1869–1938 (Harry) = Haakon VII King of Norway 1872–1957

John b and d 1871

Alexandra 1891–1959 = Arthur of Connaught 1883–1938

Olav V King of Norway 1903–

On Saturday morning, 8 March 1863, the royal yacht *Victoria and Albert* steamed up the Thames estuary bearing the Prince of Wales' lovely bride, the 18-year-old Princess Alexandra of Denmark. Although St Paul's Cathedral and Westminster Abbey had been suggested for the wedding, Queen Victoria insisted that it should be held away from public view, at St George's Chapel, Windsor. The crowd, not to be thwarted, gave the Princess the greatest welcome ever accorded to a royal bride, an enthusiasm which can only be compared to that shown on 29 July 1981, when Lady Diana Spencer was married to the present Prince of Wales.

The great welcome arose partly because the 21-year-old Prince was the first male heir to the throne in the direct line to marry since the disastrous union in 1795 of the last Prince of Wales to Caroline of Brunswick. But the British people were also delighted by her personality and beauty, and the fact that she was not a German. She would be the first future Queen not to have come from one of the German royal houses since the seventeenth century.

All along the river bank shore-batteries fired, church bells rang out, and every type of craft, from paddle steamers to rowing boats, was crammed with cheering onlookers. At Gravesend, before the royal party landed, the Prince of Wales was rowed out to the yacht to meet his bride. To the crowd's delight, he warmly kissed her.

Although it was a bitterly cold day, every available space along the railway to its terminus, at the Bricklayers' Arms station in the Old Kent Road, was jammed with spectators. Even haystacks were decorated.

After the gloom which had surrounded the Royal Family since the Prince Consort's death two years earlier, the authorities were quite unprepared for this reception, and the procession took four hours to get through the heavily congested streets to Paddington en route for Windsor. Crowds frequently blocked the way, and at the Mansion House the Prince and Princess's carriage became separated from the four others. In the confusion, a little boy was flung into a carriage to save his life, and handed over by a bewildered Danish courtier at Paddington. Lord Ronald Gower, watching in comfort at Piccadilly, said that the streets there had been densely thronged by nine in the morning. At last, after four o'clock, at a slow trot, the procession came into view. "Her lovely face has won all hearts," he wrote.

On the Princess's arrival at Windsor Castle, she was greeted by her future mother-in-law, Queen Victoria, who was dressed in deepest black; and later Alix, as she was called, went upstairs to meet en masse, for the first time, the fourteen assembled members of the Royal Family. One hinted that she was marrying Bertie for his rank and position. "No," she answered, "if he was a cowboy I should love him just the same and would marry no one else." The exuberant princess, on request, turned what must have been the first cartwheel ever to have been performed in Windsor Castle.

Queen Victoria, who watched the wedding from the privacy of the Royal Closet high above the altar, wept copiously as Jenny Lind, the "Swedish nightingale", sang a chorale for which the late Prince Consort had composed the music. To the King of Prussia, she wrote: "what a sad and dismal ceremony it was! How very different to that unforgettably beautiful one [of the Princess Royal's marriage to Prince Frederick of Prussia] on January 25th 1858. Ah, but then my mother and my angel of a husband were with me and there was nothing to mar my happiness!"

Back in London on the wedding day, the streets were still crowded by three the following morning. The theatres had flung their doors open free of charge, while in Ludgate Hill, close to St

Alix in her early twenties, photographed soon after the birth of Prince George.

Sandringham House in Norfolk, given to Bertie by his father and later greatly enlarged to its present size.

Paul's, illuminated by the new electricity, six people were killed and a hundred taken to hospital in the crush.

Alix's life had now radically changed. After a frugal upbringing in Copenhagen, where she and her younger two sisters had to do their own dressmaking, occasionally wait at table and do other household chores, she had now become the most important princess in Europe. Although her standing had improved in 1852, when her father, Prince Christian, was chosen as heir presumptive to the childless King of Denmark, this was a small and relatively unimportant country. The Glücksburg dynasty was now on the upgrade. In June, following Alix's wedding, her favourite brother, William, was chosen as the new King of Greece, adopting one of his other names as George I, after their patron saint. Then, in November, their father succeeded to the Danish throne as Christian IX. Finally, in 1866 Alix's sister Dagmar married the Tsarevitch of Russia, becoming Marie Feodorovna, later to be Tsarina and mother of the last ill-fated Tsar.

Alix was delighted with her London home, Marlborough House, and also with Sandringham which the Prince Consort had acquired for Bertie, though there were plans for rebuilding this small house in Norfolk. Immediately after the marriage there were continual rounds of entertainment which alarmed the Queen, but in September she learned with satisfaction that Alix was pregnant. An edict was issued cancelling most of her engagements.

One of Alix's constant worries was the fate of Denmark, for in December the Prussians had seized the Duchy of Holstein, part of her father's domain. Over this complex dynastic and political issue of Schleswig-Holstein, family loyalties were divided, the Queen siding with her eldest daughter in being pro-Prussian. Alix ever afterwards was fiercely "anti", as indeed was Bertie. Arguments flared up; Alix cried out in her sleep, which resulted in the Queen declaring that the subject must not be discussed in her presence. In fairness to Victoria, however, she could separate her political feelings from personal regard, and her chief criticism of the Waleses was directed at their social life.

Alix's first baby was expected in March, and preparations were planned for the birth at Marlborough House. That January, 1864, the Prince and Princess were at Frogmore House, their home at

Windsor, and the Queen at her favourite retreat of Osborne. It was a cold winter, and on the 8th Bertie and his party played a game of ice hockey on the frozen Virginia Water, where Alix was pushed along on a sledge chair. That afternoon she suffered some pain, and was eventually persuaded by her Woman of the Bedchamber, Lady Macclesfield, to return home. When they reached Frogmore at dusk, the pains grew worse. Lady Macclesfield, already the mother of twelve and expecting another, was experienced in these matters and told the Princess her time had come. After getting her into bed she sent immediately for the local doctor, Dr Brown, who unfortunately could not be located, and acquired some yards of flannel and wadding from a Windsor draper. The birth took place at 8.45 pm, only twenty minutes after Dr Brown had galloped up — a service for which he obtained a knighthood.

The Prince of Wales with his elder son, Prince Albert Victor, known as Eddy.

Thus was born the premature baby, Prince Albert Victor of Wales, who weighed three and three-quarter pounds. *Punch* came up with some verses, which contained the words:

> O hush thee, my darling, thy Sire is a Prince
> Whom Mama beheld skating not quite five hours since,
> And Grandpapa Christian is off to the fray
> With the Germans, who'd steal his nice Duchy away.

Mother and son thrived, and when six distinguished doctors arrived from London, far too late to be of use, Alix was highly amused. Within a fornight a nursery footman, Charles Fuller, was engaged, who was to spend many years of service with the family.

Six-year-old Princess Beatrice blurted out to Lady Macclesfield that her mother, the Queen, had already chosen the boy's names, Albert Victor, after her husband and herself. Alix immediately wrote: "I feel rather annoyed . . . that you had settled what our little boy was to be called before I had spoken to you about it." She scored in the end however, adding the third and fourth names — Christian Edward — and she was determined that the boy would be known as Eddy. Although careful never to come out into open conflict with the Queen, Alix nearly always managed eventually to have her own way. In the mean time society labelled the boy "All-but on the ice".

The second son, Prince George, was born at Marlborough

Prince George of Wales in 1867. The skirts were quite common wear for two-year-olds, but the hat seems eccentric by any standards. Prince George succeeded to the throne in 1910 as George V.

House on 3 June 1865, a month early. Victoria wrote: "it seems that *it is not* to be that I am to be present at the birth of your children, which I am very sorry for." This was the future King George V, whom Lady Geraldine Somerset was to call "a jolly little pickle".

Bertie wrote off to his mother: "We had both for some time settled that, if we had another boy, he should be called George, as we like the name and it is an English one." This was to be followed by Frederick. "I fear," the Queen replied, "I cannot admire the name you propose to give for the baby. I had hoped for some fine old name. Frederick is, however the best of the two, and I hope you call him so. George only came in with the Hanoverian family." (Here the Queen was wrong, for she had overlooked George, Duke of Clarence, Edward IV's and Richard III's brother who, according to tradition, was drowned in a butt of Malmsey wine.) "Of course you will add Albert at the end like your brothers, as you know we settled long ago that all dearest Papa's male descendants should bear that name to mark our line . . ." Back wrote Bertie: "We are very sorry to hear you didn't like the name that we propose to give our little boy." Georgie, as he was called, doubtless after Alix's brother, tactfully received the additional names of Ernest and Albert.

Alexandra's third pregnancy caused her to miss attending her sister Dagmar's wedding to the Tsarevitch, when she stayed with the Queen. Alix and her young sister-in-law, Princess Louise, became lifelong friends, and to her she confessed that the six weeks' absence of "her beloved one" seemed endless. Doubtless she was worrying about Bertie's fidelity, for he had to be surrounded by people who amused him, and could never settle down to a domesticated life, chatting to his wife's ladies and elderly aides. Hence came a succession of affairs which Alix had to accept, sometimes calling her husband "a naughty little man". The perceptive Queen noticed that marriage had not changed her son. "Alix is really a dear, excellent, right minded soul who one must dearly love and respect," she wrote to her daughter Vicky, but added more ominously, "I often think her lot is no easy one, but she is very fond of Bertie, though not blind."

The baby was due in March 1867. On 15 February, the day

The Princess of Wales in 1866, with her younger son Prince George on her lap, wearing the same hat. Her elder son Prince Albert Victor, later Duke of Clarence, stands by her.

The Princess of Wales carrying her eldest daughter Princess Louise — a photograph by Downey in September 1868.

the Prince left Marlborough House to attend a race meeting and dinner, Alix developed rheumatic fever. Three telegrams were sent, but he did not return until the next day to find his wife in excruciating pain in her hip and knee. Although she cried out for chloroform, the doctors decided it would be too dangerous to administer.

On the 18th it was announced that the Princess had been confined to her room, but there was "no cause for anxiety". Two days later, Louise was born, called after Alix's mother, the Queen of Denmark. Queen Victoria was not allowed to see mother and baby until a week later, when she described her daughter-in-law as "in a most pitiable state". After consulting one of the doctors, Sir William Jenner, who, she noted in her journal, was "most anxious and was very gloomy", she personally wrote to Alix's mother, Queen Louise, whom she cordially disliked, inviting her to come over.

The doctors played Alix's illness down. Bertie was convinced his wife was only suffering from post-natal depression, and was constantly out late. Lady Macclesfield, "dearest old Mac" as Alix called her, wrote that "the Princess had another bad night, chiefly owing to the Prince promising to come in at 1 pm and keeping her in a perpetual fret, refusing to take her opiate for fear she should be asleep when he came. And he never came till 3 am!"

With Alix's mother's arrival, followed two days later by her father, a wave of anxiety spread through the country, despite guarded bulletins and press reports. On their wedding anniversary, crowds outside Marlborough House grew large and menacing. Not believing the bulletins, they were convinced the Princess was dying, and as it was thought they might force an entry, an equerry had to be sent out to reassure them. After *The Times* reported, with unusual honesty, that "the inflammation was baffling to the last degree", it was fortunate for the doctors that on 20 April an improvement in Alix's condition was noticed. One of them, Sir James Paget, later admitted that her state was so critical that only her mother's appearance saved her life.

The christening took place a month later at Marlborough House, while Alix still lay in bed. When she was wheeled in for the ceremony she looked radiant, with a pink bow in her hair. That

evening, with her blessing, Bertie set off for Paris, officially to represent the Queen at Napoleon III's Great International Exhibition; but Sir William Knollys, the Prince's disapproving Comptroller, reported that he spent "supper after the opera with some of the female Paris notorieties". Soon all London knew of his neglect of his wife, the darling of the public, and on his return he was greeted with hisses and boos.

Alix's illness left her with a permanently stiff knee, but a more serious complaint was diagnosed, otosclerosis, a form of deafness inherited from her mother, and brought on by her illness and pregnancy. From this time onwards she was to become increasingly deaf. After a visit with her family to Wiesbaden for a cure, she was able to walk with two sticks, and before long she could dance, skate, ride and hunt, using a specially constructed saddle, with the pommel moved to the other side to allow for her good leg. "The Alexandra limp" was taken up by many society women.

Alix felt so well that in April 1868, despite being pregnant again, she persuaded the Queen to allow her to accompany her husband on his visit to Ireland. On 6 July Princess Victoria, known to the family as Toria, was born at Marlborough House.

That winter, Alix and Bertie went off on a long tour of northern Europe, followed by a trip via Vienna and Trieste to Egypt and the uncompleted Suez Canal. Queen Victoria had reluctantly agreed to allow them to take the two boys on the first part of the

The summer-house at Marlborough House, the London home of the Prince and Princess of Wales. The leafy silence of this corner of the garden is today drowned by the roar of traffic in the Mall.

Princess Victoria of Hesse (above), eldest daughter of Princess Alice, in 1871. She later married Prince Louis of Battenberg, and was mother of Earl Mountbatten of Burma and grandmother of Prince Philip.

tour, but she refused point blank to allow Louise to accompany them. As Alix wished to take all three to Copenhagen, she nearly cancelled the visit. The Queen told her she was being selfish, as the children "belonged to the country". After a further appeal by Bertie, the Queen gave way, on condition that the children returned from Hamburg in January. When the party reached the Nile, Eddy and Georgie wrote that they hoped their parents would not be devoured by "crockydiles", after hearing that their father had succeeded in shooting one.

Two or three hours after the travellers returned to London in mid-May 1869, Lady Geraldine Somerset was amazed to see them at the Royal Academy before going on to a court concert that evening. She would have been even more amazed had she known that Alix was once again pregnant. Princess Maud, the third and youngest daughter, arrived on 26 November at Marlborough House, also prematurely, at a very worrying time. Sir Charles Mordaunt had decided to sue for divorce after his 23-year-old wife had confessed to adultery with several men, including the Prince of Wales. Although two others were selected as co-respondents, Sir Charles behaved with great bitterness to the Prince, and threatened to subpoena him as a witness.

When the case came up in February, the Prince was called by Lady Mordaunt. He acquitted himself well after cross-examination, when he received applause, but there is no doubt that Alix was deeply hurt. She supported her husband in every way at this time, and there does not seem any basis for Sir Philip Magnus' opinion, expressed in his biography of Edward VII, that she decided to return to Denmark for a lengthy or indefinite period. Not only was this untypical of her character, but she also left long instructions that her three children's diet must not be varied until her return. As it was, she did not leave until July, escorted by Bertie, who would have remained with her but for the Queen's veto. In the event Alix returned home after a few days, on the outbreak of the Franco-Prussian War.

Her last and most difficult confinement took place in 1871. A son, John, was born on 6 April, two days after Bertie and Alix went to Sandringham for Easter. Again the birth was early; nothing was ready, and the local doctor was called in. A telegram was despatched to the Queen at Osborne to say that a son had been born, and that the Princess and her infant were "going on quite well". In the morning when Alix woke up, she was told that her baby Alexander John Charles Albert had been christened the evening before, but only lived for twenty-four hours. Although Bertie did not normally display great interest in his children, on this occasion a lady in waiting described him with "tears rolling down his cheeks". Alix watched the sad scene of her husband walking hand in hand with their two young boys in grey kilts to the simple service of burial at Sandringham.

Later that year Bertie fell critically ill from typhoid fever, an event which completely dispelled the growing movement of republicanism. Hostility to the monarchy had crossed from France, and was fanned not only by the disappearance from view of "the widow of Windsor", but also by Bertie's dissipations and extravagance, and his neglect of Alix. For her there were no more pregnancies, although she had only reached her 27th year. More and more she became bound up with her children, as Bertie turned from one mistress to another. Yet they continued to maintain a happy married life even if Bertie did get exasperated at Alix's constant unpunctuality.

Alix proved a far more devoted mother than the Queen had been. "She was in her glory," related the head nanny, Mrs Mary Blackburn, "when she could run to the nursery, put on a flannel apron, wash her children and see them asleep in their little beds. She taught them to obey their nurses and desired, in return, they should be treated with as little ceremony as possible."

Sandringham House at this time was more like an upper middle class home than those of the aristocracy, having no ancestral portraits and few heirlooms. The relationship of the Waleses to their children was equally informal. Usually parents only saw their children at set times, as they were kept almost entirely in the nursery. At Sandringham, however, the children mingled with the guests. Like their parents, they had little book learning, and as Alix was easy-going by nature and uninterested in discipline, they grew into wild and unruly children. Eddy was the exception — a backward and quiet child, with an engaging smile, similar to his mother's. Nanny Blackburn was devoted to

The Princess of Wales with her family and two dogs, in 1875. Her daughters Louise and Victoria stand on her left, and the youngest, Maud, is sitting on the ground. Her two sons, Albert Victor and George, are on her right.

59

him, and had a ring set with his first tooth between turquoises.

Both boys were smothered in mother love, calling Alix "Mother-dear" into adulthood. They constantly competed for her favours, and sometimes when driving through the park she had to sit between them to avoid a fight.

Queen Victoria found much to criticise in the *laissez-faire* manner of her grandchildren's upbringing. Remembering his own childhood, Bertie told her that "if children are too strictly or perhaps too severely treated they get shy and only fear those whom they ought to love". But commenting on Alix to her eldest

The Wales children in about 1874. Left to right, they are Princess Louise, Princess Maud, Prince Albert Victor, Prince George and Princess Victoria. In their matching nautical gear they hardly look as unruly and mischievous as they really were.

daughter, the Queen wrote: "One thing, however, she does insist on and that is great simplicity and an absence of all pride, and in that respect she has my fullest support."

The Queen sometimes found the Wales offspring "such ill-bred, ill-trained children, that I can't fancy them at all", and to the acid Lady Geraldine Somerset they were "past all management". It would be inaccurate, however, to say that Victoria always found fault. In her diary in February 1870, for instance, she noted "the dear little children, very merry in my room". Georgie was a particularly naughty boy. In April of that year, when a member of the household, Mr Collins, was playing games with them, Georgie kicked him on his shin. Mr Collins said sharply, "don't do that again", but when the boy repeated the attack Collins turned him over and gave him two sharp smacks on his behind. Georgie went red and did not cry, but never repeated the offence. There is also a famous story that Georgie once was so naughty that the Queen placed him under the table until he promised to be good. When she gave him permission to emerge, he was stark naked, to the amazement of her other guests.

'The girls were just as mischievous as their brother. One of them once lifted up her mother's train to reveal her ankles and undergarments when she was discoursing with a distinguished guest. Toria was considered the most intelligent, and showed signs of being musical, but their father preferred Georgie and the youngest, Maud. (Being something of a tomboy, Maud was nick-named Harry, after the family friend Admiral Keppel.) His backward son, Eddy, particularly annoyed him.

Their parents encouraged practical jokes, which could not have endeared them to their victims, such as squirting people with soda syphons and water-filled bicycle pumps, or making apple-pie beds. The children once coaxed a pony upstairs at Sandringham into their mother's sitting room. Alix merely said: "I was just as bad myself."

The Wales children saw much of their cousins the Tecks, to whom they were close in age. They were nearly related, because the Teck children's old grandmother, the Duchess of Cambridge, was also Alix's great-aunt. The children's mother, the Duchess of Teck, a lady of enormous girth known as "fat Mary", was fre-

The "whispering Wales" girls. Louise, Maud and Victoria, in their pony carriage about 1873.

The Duke and Duchess of Teck with three of their children. Princess May (later Queen Mary), their only daughter, sits between them. One can see why the Duchess was known as "fat Mary".

quently at Sandringham; and the two families also used to meet at Marlborough House, or at the little Palladian villa at Chiswick lent by the Duke of Devonshire to the Prince of Wales as a summer retreat from 1866 to 1879. Princess May of Teck (later Queen Mary) was three months younger than Princess Louise, and her two brothers were roughly the same age as the younger Wales princesses.

"To-day is Georgie's birthday," wrote Alix in 1870 to the Duchess of Teck. "Could not your children meet mine at Chiswick instead of coming here [Marlborough House], as I know ours like that better than playing here in the garden?" At Chiswick, round the lake, sometimes with the old Duchess of Cambridge, the "whispering Wales" girls, as they became known, romped with their "rickety old dolls" and "battered toys", for, like their mother, they were brought up to have inexpensive tastes. The boys played with wooden boats which had been made for them by a footman.

The Duchess of Teck was one of the few who called the Wales girls "the dear little trio" (they all dressed alike). "I have been in the nursery," she wrote from Sandringham in February 1873, to "her chicks". "Looloo, Victoria and sweet tiny Maudie have been showing me all their pretty picture books, after which I assisted at their tea."

When the boys were respectively aged 7 and nearly 6, Queen Victoria selected a tutor, the Rev John Neale Dalton, the 32-year-old curate of Whippingham, her parish church at Osborne. With a first class honours degree in Theology at Cambridge, he proved a success, and managed to establish an orderly routine. He could make little headway with the lethargic Eddy, but he retained the Queen's faith in his abilities, and reported any progress to her at regular intervals. He also managed to gain the boys' confidence. Georgie later described a spot in the grounds at Sandringham: "It was here that Dalton used to teach us to shoot with bow and arrow, and down there that he ran when he allowed us to shoot at him as the running deer."

Although Georgie was an average pupil, it may be that Eddy's backwardness resulted from a physical defect. Sir Henry Ponsonby, Queen Victoria's Private Secretary, observed that the boy "is a little deaf". Perhaps Dalton's booming voice, noted when he later became a Canon of St George's Chapel, resulted from this time. Michael Harrison, in his biography of Eddy, who became the Duke of Clarence, suggested that the boy may have suffered from "petit mal", a mild form of epilepsy associated with migraine, which usually emerges with puberty but disappears with the end of adolescence, sometimes to recur later in life.

The Princes worked hard under Dalton, with preparation before breakfast and before bed, leaving afternoons free for games or riding. He himself taught them everything except for French, for which they had a separate tutor, and carefully kept albums to show their progress or otherwise.

The Prince of Wales was able to persuade Queen Victoria to agree to the Princes being sent to the *Britannia* "as an experiment", and after passing their entrance examination in 1877 when they were aged thirteen and twelve, they joined the ship that November accompanied by Mr Dalton. Here they remained for nearly two years before going on an extended cruise in the *Bacchante*, again with Mr Dalton, for a further three.

In May 1890 Queen Victoria created her eldest grandson, Eddy, Duke of Clarence. Unstable in character, Eddy fell in and out of love several times, once seriously with Princess Hélène, daughter of the Comte de Paris. Their prospective marriage bristled with difficulties: politically because, although France was a republic,

Chiswick House, the Palladian villa designed by Lord Burlington in 1725, where the Wales and Teck children played together in the 1870s.

Princess Mary of Wales in about 1910. She later married Lord Lascelles, 6th Earl of Harewood, and became Princess Royal in 1932, after the death of her aunt Louise.

the Comte was Pretender to the French throne; and religiously because he was a staunch Roman Catholic. After much persuasion, supported by Alix, Queen Victoria privately allowed the engagement to stand when the Prime Minister, Lord Salisbury, was consulted; but it came to naught because her father would not allow Hélène to change her faith without the Pope's consent. Although she visited the Pope, Leo XIII, deadlock ensued.

Hélène's love for Eddy was one-sided, because he was already writing love-letters to Lady Sybil St Clair-Erskine, sister of the Earl of Rosslyn. His mother knew nothing of this development, according to Georgina Battiscombe's *Queen Alexandra*. "To her he was simply her lovesick boy over whom her heart constantly grieved."

A year after the Princess Hélène debacle, the Duke's engagement to Princess May of Teck was announced. "Beloved Mama," Alix wrote to Queen Victoria, "I do hope Eddy has found the *right bride*" — whom she then proceeded to praise to the skies. The Queen agreed, and the wedding day was fixed for 27 February 1892. On 4 January May and her parents went to Sandringham for her fiancé's 28th birthday. Four days later Eddy succumbed to influenza, pneumonia set in and on 14 January he was dead.

Now the second place in the direct line of succession to the throne fell to his only brother Georgie, who was made Duke of York in the following May. In 1910 he succeeded his father, Edward VII, to the throne as King George V.

Princess Louise, at the age of 22, became engaged to Lord Fife, eighteen years her senior. She expected some opposition. Princess May, writing to her Aunt Augusta, reflected the general attitude of a non-royal alliance by saying "we are very glad for her because she has liked him for some years, but for a future Princess Royal to marry a subject seems rather strange, don't you think". Queen Victoria gave Louise her consent, and wrote in her diary, "it is a very brilliant marriage in a worldly point of view as he is immensely rich". In July 1889 the couple married quietly in the chapel at Buckingham Palace. Two days after the wedding the bridegroom was created Duke of Fife.

Louise, highly strung, nervous and often ailing, had no wish to succeed to the crown which was now perilously near. On Eddy's death only one life stood between her and this eventuality on her father's death — that of her unmarried brother, Georgie; and it was she who played a large part in bringing him together with May. This was a delicate problem for one so recently bereaved. It was at Louise's house of Sheen Lodge, near Richmond, that their engagement was announced. In 1905 Louise, as the Sovereign's eldest daughter, was declared to be the Princess Royal.

In December 1911, when Louise's brother had succeeded as George V, she, her husband and their two daughters, aged 20 and 18, left to winter in Egypt for her health. The ship went aground in heavy seas off the Moroccan coast, and their lifeboat also sank. They floated about in lifebelts until they were saved by Admiral Cradock, but even after the little band of survivors landed on the beach their ordeal was not over. Suffering from cold and shock they trecked five miles to reach mules to carry them to Tangier. As they appeared none the worse, they continued their journey to Egypt; but by an irony of fate at Assuan, during a trip up the Nile, it was the Duke, weakened by the shipwreck, who contracted pleurisy and died.

During the remaining twenty years of Louise's life, she became almost a recluse at her London house in Portman Square. By the time she died there in January 1931, most of the public had forgotten that she had ever existed.

The second daughter, Princess Victoria, had two romances, but neither of her would-be suitors would in those days have been an acceptable royal consort. One is said to have been a member of the Baring family who had relations in the Household, and the other her father's equerry, Sir Arthur Davidson. Even the Prime Minister, Lord Rosebery, a widower nineteen years her senior, thought of marrying her. Alix was appalled.

By 1894 Queen Victoria was most concerned that neither Victoria nor Maud showed any signs of marrying, but the principal reason for their continued spinsterhood was that their mother could not bear to part with them. In that year the Queen wrote to Vicky suggesting Prince Dolly of Teck, May's eldest brother, for one of them, but her daughter did not think that he was good enough for a British princess. In any case he soon found another bride. Vicky concluded: "it really is not *wise* to leave the fate of these dear

Princess Alice of Albany, who married the Earl of Athlone and died in 1981 at the age of 98.

Three of Beatrice's children by Prince Henry of Battenberg — from the left, Prince Leopold, Prince Alexander and Princess Ena — in 1891.

girls — dans le vague!" The Queen approached Bertie, who said he was powerless.

The Crown Prince of Denmark came to London that summer, and the Queen approached Alix about this nephew of hers. Alix agreed he would make a suitable husband, but she was afraid "the girls thought him too young for them".

Victoria remained the dutiful unmarried daughter of Alix as Princess of Wales, as Queen (in 1901), and as Queen Dowager (in 1910), fetching and carrying at her mother's whim; for as she grew older Alix became selfish and forgetful. "Poor Toria was just a glorified maid to her mother," wrote a Russian cousin.

After her mother's death in 1925, Victoria settled down at Coppins, in Buckinghamshire, where she died in December 1935. The loss of this favourite sister of George V proved a blow from which he never recovered, for he only survived her by six weeks. John Gore, in his book *King George V*, told of their daily telephone conversations. "Every morning I rang up my sister at half past nine, just to have a chat," the King said. "Of course we are not always too polite. One morning her telephone bell rang at the usual time, and she took up the receiver and said, 'Hullo, you old fool,' and the voice of the operator broke in, 'Beg pardon, Your Royal Highness, His Majesty is not yet on the line.'"

In 1895, a year after the Crown Prince of Denmark's visit,

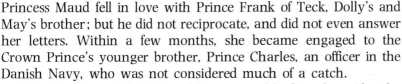

Princess Maud fell in love with Prince Frank of Teck, Dolly's and May's brother; but he did not reciprocate, and did not even answer her letters. Within a few months, she became engaged to the Crown Prince's younger brother, Prince Charles, an officer in the Danish Navy, who was not considered much of a catch.

The Duchess of Teck found him a good-looking boy, "but he looks *fully 3 years younger* than Maud, had *no money*, they are not going either to give him a house". However, the marriage did take place at Buckingham Palace in July 1896, and in 1905 Maud found herself unexpectedly a Queen. Charles was elected King of Norway on its separation from Sweden, when he took the title of Haakon VII.

As a gift from her father, Queen Maud received Appleton House on the Sandringham estate, which was to remain hers for life, and it was here she gave birth to her only child, King Olav V, the present King of Norway, who has remained a frequent visitor to Britain. Queen Maud died in 1938 while undergoing an operation in a London nursing home, and before her burial she was taken to the little chapel at Marlborough House where she had been christened.

None of Edward VII's children had the stamina of the previous generation, and when Maud, the last of them, died, three of Queen Victoria's were still living.

Four of Affie's children — Marie, Victoria Melita, Alexandra and Young Alfred of Edinburgh — in 1881.

The Princess of Wales, Alix, with her grandson Prince Edward in about 1895.

George V's Children

"My father was frightened of his mother;
I was frightened of my father, and I am
damned well going to see to it that my
children are frightened of me."
— George V

*George and Mary, Duke and
Duchess of York, with their
young family in Scotland in
1906. From the left, the
children are Princess Mary,
Prince Henry, Prince George,
Prince John (who lived only
another twelve years), Prince
Edward (Edward VIII) and
Prince Albert (George VI).*

The wedding of Prince George to May of Teck in July 1893. Among the numerous bridesmaids are his sisters Victoria and Maud (standing, right). The others are his cousins of Edinburgh, Schleswig-Holstein, Connaught and Battenberg.

Prince Edward, who became Edward VIII and then Duke of Windsor, aged about four.

The two brothers, Edward and Albert, in 1896.

Edward, Albert and Mary of York, in 1900.

Prince Edward wheeling his brother Albert (George VI).

Edward, Albert and Mary, with their two-year-old brother Henry and their grandfather the King; and (opposite) artfully posing for a studio photograph.

74

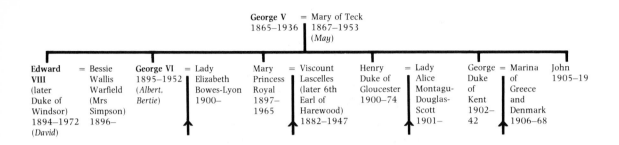

				George V = Mary of Teck							
				1865–1936 1867–1953							
				(May)							

Edward VIII (later Duke of Windsor) 1894–1972 (David) = Bessie Wallis Warfield (Mrs Simpson) 1896–   George VI 1895–1952 (Albert, Bertie) = Lady Elizabeth Bowes-Lyon 1900–   Mary Princess Royal 1897–1965 = Viscount Lascelles (later 6th Earl of Harewood) 1882–1947   Henry Duke of Gloucester 1900–74 = Lady Alice Montagu-Douglas-Scott 1901–   George Duke of Kent 1902–42 = Marina of Greece and Denmark 1906–68   John 1905–19

Princess Marie of Edinburgh, Queen Victoria's first choice as a wife for Prince George, when she was aged nine. In 1914 she became Queen of Roumania.

After Eddy's death in January 1892, now that his brother George was destined for the throne, there was immediate concern about the royal succession. Queen Victoria's first choice for a bride for George was another of her grandchildren, 16-year-old Princess Marie of Edinburgh, known as Missy. George, a 26-year-old naval officer, was eager for this match; but when a formal offer was made Missy's mother, the Duchess of Edinburgh, flatly turned it down: instead the girl was soon married off to Ferdinand, later King of Roumania. Queen Victoria then decided that the most suitable wife for her grandson would be the recently bereaved Princess May of Teck, who was barely recovering from the death of her fiancé Eddy.

In May the Queen created George a duke. Bertie wished for York, the traditional title for the second son, although the Queen disliked this name because it had been borne by one of her wicked Hanoverian uncles. She suggested London, but Bertie had his way. All eyes now turned to May, who so recently was to have become the Duchess of Clarence. "From London I hear that the Queen downwards are resolved P. George should marry May!" Lady Geraldine Somerset wrote in her diary, "all except P. George!" James Pope-Hennessy, in his *Queen Mary*, adds that if she had been acquainted with facts instead of idle gossip, she would have said

"All, except Princess May".

The situation must have aroused May of Teck's acute embarrassment. She had to face not only broad hints from her mother, the Duchess of Teck, but also intense speculation in the press. At first the Prince and Princess of Wales were hostile to the plan. Queen Victoria told Sir Henry Ponsonby that the Prince "must not prevent the marriage. Something dreadful will happen if he does not marry". In reality the two people concerned were attracted to each other, and united in grief. Eventually when, in May 1893, Princess May visited Sheen Lodge, Princess Louise's Richmond home, she found Prince George was staying there with his sister. "Now, Georgie," Princess Louise laughingly told her brother, "don't you think you ought to take May into the garden to look at the frogs in the pond?" When the two returned to the house, they announced their engagement.

The wedding took place at the Chapel Royal, St James's Palace, on 6 July, after which the bridal pair travelled to Sandringham to their new home. This was the Bachelor's Cottage, now renamed York Cottage in their honour, which had been given to them by the Prince and Princess of Wales as a wedding present.

York Cottage was a small house surrounded by shrubs and trees, a quarter of a mile from Sandringham House, always known as the big house, and had been built by the Prince for an overflow of guests at his many house parties. Princess Alice, Countess of Athlone, described it as "a poky and inconvenient place, architecturally repulsive and always full of the smell of cooking. George adored it, but then he had the only convenient room in the house, which was called the 'Library', though it contained very few books. . . . The drawing room was small enough when only two adults occupied it – but after tea, when five children were crammed into it as well, it became a veritable bedlam".

This was to become the happy home of the Duke and Duchess of York for 33 years, although May did find it too small. "Never live in a hutch," she once told a friend. They were as one in their feelings about their London home, York House, part of St James's Palace, without a single sunny room and no private entrance. In 1895, George told his wife it is "a beastly house & I think very unhealthy".

To May's chagrin both homes had already been furnished with the aid of Maple's, for this well-educated Princess was both artistic and knowledgeable about antiques. John Gore, in his *King George V, a Personal Memoir*, wrote that "she was living in a small house on an estate which drew its inspiration wholly from the Prince and Princess [of Wales], whereon every smallest happening or alteration was ordered and taken note of by the Prince. The very arrangement of her rooms, the planting of her small garden, were matters which required reference to Sandringham House, and the smallest innovation would be regarded with distrust". That May could live there without exhibiting any rift was a tribute to her extreme tact.

It was intended that the first child should have been born at Buckingham Palace in mid-June 1894, but as it was a hot summer May persuaded her doctors that she should go for her first confinement to her parents' home at White Lodge in Richmond Park, away from public view. Accordingly, the two moved in on the 4th. When days went by with no news the Royal Family became restive. "Dear May keeps us waiting a little, but it must be very soon," Queen Victoria wrote, and May's Aunt Augusta told the Duchess of Teck: "No telegram about dear May! We had so reckoned upon it so each time the door went open we jumped up, hoping."

At last, at ten in the evening of 23 June, a son was born. Aunt Augusta (Grand Duchess of Mecklenburg-Strelitz) summed up the attitude of all the family: "I still am in a *twitter*, can hardly take in the immense happiness of the moment."

Queen Victoria came over from Windsor on the 27th with Princess Beatrice and several others of her family to inspect her new great-grandson, taking a special train to Richmond. She was duly impressed with "a vy fine strong boy, a pretty child". To her daughter Vicky, the Empress Frederick, she wrote: "It seems that it has never happened in this Country that there shd be 3 direct Heirs as well as the Sovereign alive."

There was the usual wrangle about names. Queen Victoria wanted the boy to be called Prince Albert, but her grandson, George, Duke of York, wrote: "Ever since I can remember I have always tried my best to be a dutiful grandson to you and never go

Four monarchs, four generations. Queen Victoria is with her son the Prince of Wales (Edward VII) and her grandson the Duke of York (George V), and has her great grandson Edward, the future Edward VIII and then Duke of Windsor, on her lap.

Queen Victoria with her great grandson, Prince Edward of York. This was the first occasion that there was an heir in the direct line for three generations.

against your wishes. Long before our dear child was born, both May and I settled that if it was a boy we should call him Edward after darling Eddy. *This is the dearest wish of our hearts*, dearest Grandmama . . ." The Queen, unwillingly, acquiesced, although she added, "you write as if *Edward* was the real name of dear Eddy, while it was *Albert Victor*".

Prince Edward, who had twelve sponsors, was christened in the White Lodge drawing room with the names of Edward Albert Christian George Andrew Patrick David. It was the last of these that the family called him; and the public interest which had, so far, missed his father, now focussed upon him and followed him for the rest of his days.

During George's and May's long stay at White Lodge, he found his mother-in-law very tiring. Subsequently pouring out his heart to May during her absence with her mother at St Moritz, he told her: "I am very fond of dear Maria [his name for the Duchess], but I assure you I wouldn't go through the six weeks I spent at White Lodge again for anything. She used to come in & disturb us & then her unpunctuality used to annoy me too dreadfully. She was always most kind to me & therefore it made it impossible for me to say anything." May agreed. "I know how true it is, & it used to fidget me dreadfully when I was laid up to feel that we could hardly ever be alone without being interrupted." When eighteen months later the next birth was imminent they took good care that it should be at Sandringham, and that the Duchess of Teck was not to be invited until a few days later.

The proud father entered in his diary, "a little boy weighing nearly 8 pounds at 9.40 (S.T.) evening, most satisfactory . . ." (S.T. signified Sandringham time, where the Prince of Wales advanced all clocks by half an hour, not, as is sometimes believed, to compensate for Alix's perpetual unpunctuality, but to give extra daylight for shooting.) The birth could not have occurred on a more inauspicious day, 10 December 1895, for this was the anniversary both of the Prince Consort's and his daughter Princess Alice's deaths – Mausoleum Day, as the Royal Family called it, after the annual service at Frogmore which all were obliged to attend.

The Prince of Wales thought it would be diplomatic for his son to call the baby Albert, which delighted the Queen. The boy was christened at St Mary's, Sandringham, with the names Albert Frederick Arthur George, but known as Bertie, like his grandfather. The baby's grandmother, the Duchess of Teck, however, told her son Alge (later Earl of Athlone) that she hoped the last name "may supplant the less favoured one"; this was prophetic, for when Bertie succeeded to the throne in 1936 it was as King George VI.

At the christening, just before the actual baptism when Bertie lay in the arms of the Bishop of Norwich, he let out a tremendous yell which started off his brother, who had to be removed to the vestry.

Like Bertie, all the subsequent York children were born at York Cottage, Sandringham. On 25 April 1897, Diamond Jubilee Year, May gave birth to her only daughter, christened Victoria Alexandra Alice Mary, but always known by her last name. Perhaps fortunately, her grandfather's idea that she should be called Diamond was abandoned. Mary was to prove the brightest of the family. Her eldest brother once said that it was a pity she would not succeed, for "she was much cleverer than me".

When Prince Henry was born on 31 March 1900, during the Boer War, the C-in-C, Lord Roberts, was invited to be a sponsor, and sent his acceptance from Bloemfontein. May told her aunt, "I confess I am just a little bit proud of myself for having produced another boy which was greatly wished, as alas we have so few princes in our family now. I think I have done my duty and may now *stop*, as having babies is highly distasteful to me tho' when once they are there they are very nice! The children are pleased with the new baby who they think flew in at my window & had to have his wings cut off!" But despite May's distaste, which reminds one of the similar views expressed by Queen Victoria years before, two more children were yet to appear.

Prince George was born five days before Christmas in 1902, and after a gap came Prince John, on 12 July 1905. "I shall soon have a regiment not a family," said their father at the former's birth. These two youngest children were born in the reign of their grandfather, King Edward VII, who succeeded Queen Victoria in 1901.

The Prince of Wales (Duke of Windsor) in his sailor suit, carrying his brother Prince George.

York Cottage was adapted to contain two small rooms up-stairs for the day and night nurseries, separated from the re-mainder by a swing door. "When there were three of us," David recalled when he was Duke of Windsor, "we all slept there with a nurse." Their favourite nanny, Mrs Bill, whom they called Lalla, later told him, indicating with a wave of the hand her modest

Two young York children with their nurse Mrs Bill, the beloved Lalla, in about 1900. Princess Mary is behind Lalla, who is holding Prince Henry (later Duke of Gloucester).

Queen Alexandra with her Wales grandchildren, in Scotland around 1905. She is holding Prince George of Wales (Duke of Kent), and in the foreground are, from the left, Prince Albert (George VI), Prince Henry (Duke of Gloucester), and Princess Mary (Princess Royal).

suburban living room, that the Day Nursery "was only about half as big as this. There was very little room for toys in it. You had only one small rocking horse. Perhaps it was a good thing your sister didn't go for dolls. They would have cluttered the place up terribly".

The first nanny was dismissed for rudeness to the Duchess of Teck, and her successor was a sadistic monster. The Duke of Windsor wrote in his memoirs that this "dreadful 'nanny' would pinch and twist my arm — why no one knew unless it was to demonstrate, according to some perverse reasoning, that her power over me was greater than that of my parents. The sobbing and bawling this treatment invariably evoked understandably puzzled, worried and finally annoyed them. It would result in my being peremptorily removed from the room before further embarrassment was inflicted upon them and the other witnesses of this pathetic scene".

Prince Albert (George VI) aged two.

This nanny made it clear that David was her favourite charge, and she treated the second, Bertie, with the utmost neglect. She used to give him his bottle-feed while driving in a C-spring Victoria, from which he developed chronic stomach trouble, which may well have been the root cause of his later illness. Eventually the boys' mother discovered her cruelty and inefficiency and dismissed her. She was replaced by the beloved Lalla, who had been under-nurse to her two predecessors and with whom they always kept in touch.

Prince Albert, by nature a shy and reserved child, was rather prone to tears. Both boys were terrified by their father's abrupt quarter-deck manner, which the Duke of Windsor called a "gruff blue water approach to all human problems". Although he liked to play with his children when they were babies — "I made a very good lap," he told one of his wife's ladies — he had little patience with them subsequently, apart from his favourite, Princess Mary. "Now you are five years old," he told Bertie, "I hope you will always try & be obedient & do at once what you are told, as you will find it will come much easier to you the sooner you begin. I always tried to do this when I was your age & found it made me much happier." He was evidently quite oblivious to his own extreme naughtiness at the same age. "No words that I was ever

The new Prince George, born in 1902, being inspected by his brothers and sister. By this time their father had become Prince of Wales (later George V). From the left they are Prince Albert (George VI), Prince Henry, Princess Mary and Prince Edward.

to hear could be so disconcerting to the spirit as the summons, usually delivered by a footman, that 'His Royal Highness wishes to see you in the Library'. My father's study was in a sense his Captain's Cabin, and one never knew on being summoned there what one might be in for. . . . He might wish to show some stamps. . . . . But more often we would be called to account for some alleged act of misbehaviour. Bertie and I — mostly I — came in for a good deal of scolding for being late or dirty, for making a noise on some solemn occasion. . . . And inevitably, just as my mother's room came to represent a kind of sanctuary at the end of the day, so the Library became for us the seat of parental authority, the place of admonition and reproof."

Mabell, Countess of Airlie, one of May's ladies in waiting, said that they have often been depicted as stern and unloving parents, but this they most certainly were not. "The tragedy was that neither had any understanding of a child's mind. . . . Prince George was fond of his sons but his manner to them alternated between an awkward jocularity of the kind which makes a sensitive child squirm from self-consciousness and a severity bordering on harshness."

When Queen Victoria died in 1901, Prince George, now heir apparent, automatically became Duke of Cornwall and York. Months went by and the new King did not create him Prince of Wales, the usual title for the eldest son. Princess May wrote to her confidante and former nanny, Hélène Bricka, a highly-educated lady who had once been her mother's companion, "I don't think they intend to create G. Pce of Wales". Then, on King Edward's birthday, he gave in and his son received the title. It was thought that Alix was against its disposal, as she and Bertie had been known as such ever since their wedding. Afterwards she always addressed May as "Her Royal Highness Victoria Mary Princess of Wales", and never as the Princess of Wales.

The change of sovereigns also meant a change of homes. Marlborough House was to be vacated by the new King, but it was not until the spring of 1903 that the new Prince and Princess of Wales could take possession. Alix clung on as long as she could, and wrote to her son of "tearing myself away from the old House . . . that I feel will finish me!" Strangely enough, even May had by

then become attached to York House.

In 1902 King Edward made over Frogmore House in the Home Park at Windsor to his son and daughter-in-law. This delighted them. "It is too divine here," wrote May to her husband, "and everything is looking lovely. The house charming & fresh & the garden & grounds a dream." Here beside the lake the children played. Then there was Abergeldie Castle on Deeside, where the Prince could indulge his passion for deer-stalking and grouse-shooting. In these two houses, when their father was sailing at Cowes or engaged in shooting, the children could occasionally be alone with their mother, and were at their happiest.

Less than two months after Queen Victoria's death, the Prince and Princess of Wales set out for a tour of the British Empire in the *Orphir*, and were away for nearly eight months. The children were left in the care of their grandparents, who spoilt them tremendously. They moved from Marlborough House to Sandringham with their governesses and nurses, and in the summer went to Osborne, so soon to be a convalescent home, and to Balmoral. Their lessons were given by Mlle Bricka, now elderly and plump, of whom May was so fond. She frequently waited patiently upstairs for her charges to arrive. As the Duke of Windsor recalled: "If we were too long in going she would enter the dining-room timidly to warn us that we were already late for our afternoon

*Prince Edward and Princess
Mary in 1901.*

lesson. Usually my grandmother would wave her away, and my grandfather, puffing at his cigar, might add reassuringly . . . 'it's all right, let the children stay a little longer. We shall send them upstairs presently.'"

When the children were later taken to Sandringham, Mlle Bricka was left behind so as not to spoil the fun, and she wrote to complain to May. Queen Alexandra explained that they did not take Bricka because Sir Francis Laking, one of the doctors, particularly asked that Edward "might be left more with his brothers and sisters *for a little while* as *we all* noticed how precocious and *old-fashioned* he was getting".

After the Prince and Princess of Wales returned from their tour in the autumn of 1901, David and Bertie were placed in the charge of Frederick Finch, who had already served three years as a nursery footman, and Lalla became exclusively Mary's nurse. It had been decided that the two elder boys would follow the example of their father and Eddy by entering the Navy. Accordingly, a tutor was to be hired until they were old enough to become cadets, and in the spring of 1902 Henry Peter Hansell, a pipe-smoking bachelor from Norfolk, was engaged. The boys called him "Mider" (from "mister").

According to Sir John Wheeler-Bennett, Mr Hansell was fully conscious of his inadequacies for the task, and soon decided that the boys would benefit by a school education. In this he was over-ruled, and instead he set up a school room on the second floor of York Cottage, to which he brought standard desks, a blackboard and wall maps. The boys had to be at their desks by 7.30 in the morning for three quarters of an hour's prep before breakfast. By 9 o'clock they were back at work until lunchtime, with an hour's break for play. After lunch there would be a walk, then lessons for another hour until teatime, the last meal of the day; then more work until 6.30, when the children went to their mother's boudoir for a chat or to be read to. Mr Hansell's uninspired syllabus hardly concerned literature or the arts, but their father's attitude to his sons was, "the Navy will teach them all they will want to know".

Princess Mary came under Mr Hansell's authority for a short time. "I must keep Princess Mary apart from the others as much as possible," he reported, "whenever it is a matter of work. Her disposition is mercurial; one can enforce discipline . . . but the fact remains that, so long as she is in the room, her brothers cannot concentrate their attention on any serious work."

A French governess, Mlle José Dussau, a stricter disciplinarian than either Finch or Mr Hansell, was brought in, and she made it compulsory to speak French at meal times. Although Mary adored her, the boys rebelled, and as a result a French tutor, M. Gabriel Hua, who had once taught their father, was also engaged, and appointed Librarian.

David left home in 1907 to become a cadet at Osborne. Henry now succeeded him in the school room. "Prince Albert is now the head boy," reported Mr Hansell in May. "I am very glad to say that Prince Albert gives promise of taking a serious and sensible view of his responsibilities," but by December he reported: "he has failed to appreciate his position as 'captain'." Not only did Bertie intensely dislike maths, but he had to endure many problems of health. At his 7th or 8th year, his stammering began, an affliction which is now thought to have arisen from his being forced as a left-handed boy to write with his right hand. Also, like his younger brother Henry, he suffered from being knock-kneed, and Sir Francis Laking devised a series of splints. For a time the boys had both to work and to sleep in them, and their work was certainly affected. "Practically all Prince Albert's work with me has been combined with the splints," Hansell reported, and in 1904 he wrote: "it is now quite certain that such a combination is impossible."

Many found Bertie the most engaging of the children. Lady Airlie, for instance, felt that "the child to whom I was most drawn was Albert — Bertie — although he was not a boy who made friends easily. Intensively sensitive over his stammer, he was apt to take refuge either in silence — which caused him to be thought moody or in naughtiness. He made his first shy overture to me at Easter 1902 — after I had been only a few weeks in the Household — when he presented me with an Easter card. It was his own work, and very well done for a child of six — a design of spring flowers and chicks, evidently cut out from a magazine, coloured in crayons, and pasted on a cardboard. He was so anxious for me to receive

Prince Albert of York (George VI) photographed in 1901 in his sailor suit.

it in time for Easter that he decided to deliver it in person. He waylaid me one morning when I came out of his mother's boudoir, but at the last moment his courage failed him, and thrusting the card into my hand without a word he darted away". Later his father told her: "Bertie has more guts than the rest of his brothers put together."

Prince Henry's poor health prevented him from entering the Royal Naval College like his brothers. Laking offered his home at York Gate House, by the sea at Broadstairs, for the boy, and Sister Edith Ward who had once nursed the doctor was brought in to look after the Prince, who started there in February 1910. As Henry proved backward and prone to crying, Sister Ward recommended that he should enter Mr Richardson's school at St Peter's Court nearby. Sister Ward remained to look after him, taking him to school daily. But after a few days, Prince Henry agreed he would like to become a boarder. In 1912, when he returned for the summer term, he was accompanied there by his next brother, Prince George, who though three years his junior quickly rivalled his performance in class. Prince Henry thus became the first son of a King to be educated at school, and he later entered Eton. Prince George followed his brothers as a naval cadet.

The youngest of the children, Prince John, was an amusing little child, but unfortunately when he was young he developed epilepsy. He was a special favourite of his grandmother, Queen Alexandra, and her letters are full of references to him. She often used to send for "the dear and precious little boy" to have him over to play games or listen to music.

His condition deteriorated, and by a decision made when he had reached the age of 11, he was removed from home and taken to Wood Farm, Wolferton, near Sandringham, to be looked after exclusively by Mrs Bill and a man servant. "We dare not let him be with his brothers and sister because it upset them so much," Lalla said. "With the attacks getting so bad and coming so often, what else could we do." John died in his 14th year, on 18 January 1919, and was quietly buried at Sandringham. "Now our two darling Johnnies lie side by side," wrote Alix to her daughter-in-law, May, remembering her own son of this name who had died after twenty-four hours.

In May 1910, George and May, Prince and Princess of Wales, became King George V and Queen Mary, on the death of his father Edward VII. Sandringham House was to remain Queen Alexandra's until her death in 1925. Despite some criticism that she did not move to York Cottage when she was left a widow, her son always said "it is my mother's house. My father built it for her".

George V was virtually unknown to the public until he became king. His father's glittering court had vanished. His own was essentially respectable, which many in society considered dull. Nevertheless the quiet and happy family life of the King and Queen, combined with their strong sense of duty, made them ideal constitutional monarchs. Although they were tied by a strong bond of affection, both were unable to express themselves except on paper. When the King wrote to tell her of his love and admiration to "his sweet Angel May", she wrote in reply, "what a pity it is you cannot *tell* me what you write, for I should appreciate it so

George V and Queen Mary on the balcony of Buckingham Palace, acknowledging the cheers of the crowd on their Silver Jubilee in May 1935. Between them are Princess Elizabeth and (peeping over the parapet) Princess Margaret of York.

Queen Mary holding the newly born Princess Elizabeth of York (Elizabeth II) in 1926.

enormously. It is such a blessing to know that I am a help to you".

Neither had any idea of the popularity which surrounded them at the time of their Silver Jubilee in May 1935. "The greatest number of people in the streets I have ever seen in my life," said King George. "I'd no idea they felt like that about me. I am beginning to think they must really like me for myself." He had been seriously ill in 1929, and eight months after the Jubilee, on 27 January 1936, he died at Sandringham — "the place I love better than anywhere else in the world".

Queen Mary, a regal figure, is today remembered for her old-fashioned clothes and toque. The fact that year after year she never changed with the fashion owed a great deal to the Victorian views of her husband. There was another side to her, however, for Lady Airlie told of her sense of fun, "carefully controlled like all her emotions". She laughed over jokes in *La Vie Parisienne*, sent comic postcards to her friends (in an envelope), learned the words of "Yes, We Have No Bananas", the hit of 1923, "and singing it with me at the top of our voices for the joy of shocking a particularly staid member of the Household; hopping in a green and white brocade dress round one of the drawing-rooms at Windsor to represent a grasshopper in a game of Dumb Crambo after dinner. She was not always the dignified Queen Consort known to the world".

Queen Mary suffered great distress when her eldest son David, who in January 1936 became King Edward VIII, sacrificed his throne in order to marry the divorcée Mrs Wallis Simpson, and after an eleven months' reign sailed to exile on the continent. His successor was Bertie, who had been created Duke of York before his happy marriage in 1923 to Lady Elizabeth Bowes-Lyon, daughter of the Earl of Strathmore. Now George VI, the third monarch to reign in that fateful year, he created his brother Duke of Windsor. Appalled at the prospect of reigning with no training, and overcoming great difficulties, a serious voice impediment and poor health, King George VI nevertheless became one of the most loved British monarchs of all time. For this he gave much of the credit to his wife, now the Queen Mother.

World War II broke out less than three years after he came to the throne. In 1942 Queen Mary was to lose her youngest surviving son George, Duke of Kent, in an air crash in Scotland when he was serving in the RAF as an air commodore. Prince George had inherited his mother's artistic gifts, and as collectors the two used to make frequent expeditions to antique shops. Like the present Prince Andrew, he was the royal "pin-up" of his time. "There are hundreds of charming creatures throughout the country," said Edgar Wallace, "who have a portrait of Prince George on their bedroom walls and can hardly keep their eyes off it." His beautiful wife, Princess Marina of Greece and Denmark, was a great-niece of Queen Alexandra.

Princess Elizabeth with her parents.

The last great emotional shock that Queen Mary suffered was the death in February 1952 of her second son, George VI. Her granddaughter, the new Queen Elizabeth II, flew back from Kenya the next day, and Queen Mary drove to Clarence House that afternoon to pay her homage. "Her old Granny and subject must be the first to kiss her hand," she said.

At Queen Mary's own death on 24 March 1953, aged 85 years, she was the queen who had lived the longest in our history. Her last wish was that mourning for her should not postpone the coronation scheduled for 2 June.

Three other children survived her. Princess Mary, who had served as a nurse with the VAD in World War I and at Great Ormond Street hospital until 1920, had been the first to marry. Her wedding took place at Westminster Abbey in 1922 to Viscount Lascelles, later 6th Earl of Harewood, and ten years later she was declared Princess Royal, her aunt Princess Louise, Duchess of Fife, who held this title, having died in the previous year, 1931. The Princess Royal died suddenly and unexpectedly in the garden of Harewood House, Yorkshire, in March 1965.

The Duke of Windsor's long exile in France lasted until his death in May 1972. His brother Prince Henry, Duke of Gloucester, whose service as a full-time army officer abruptly ended on his brother's abdication, married Lady Alice Montagu-Douglas-Scott, daughter of the Duke of Buccleuch and Queensberry. He survived for two further years, but a severe stroke had rendered him speechless. Both brothers, after ceremonial funerals at St George's Chapel, Windsor, lie buried with other members of the Royal Family at Frogmore, near where they had once played as happy children.

George VI's Children

"He has one matchless blessing, enjoyed
by so many of you and not bestowed
on me, a happy home with his wife and
children." — Edward VIII

*Queen Elizabeth with her
daughters, Princess Elizabeth and
Princess Margaret, in 1936.
This was the year in which
George V died, Edward VIII
abdicated and George VI
ascended the throne.*

*The future Queen Elizabeth II
at the age of two.*

*The young princesses were both
taught to ride at the express
wish of their grandfather,
George V. They are pictured here
with an assistant to Mr Owen,
the King's stud groom.*

94

Princess Elizabeth looks rather exasperated at being delayed on her way to St Paul's to celebrate the Silver Jubilee of her grandfather's reign, on 6 May 1935. With her is Princess Margaret.

Inside St Paul's at the Silver Jubilee ceremony. Princess Elizabeth is bending down to see the crowds outside the cathedral. Behind stand the Duke of York, Archbishop Lang, and the Duke of Kent. In front is the Duchess of York.

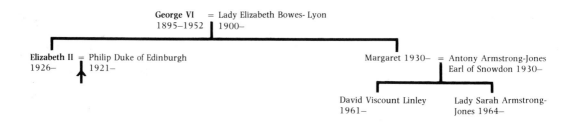

George VI = Lady Elizabeth Bowes- Lyon
1895–1952   1900–

Elizabeth II = Philip Duke of Edinburgh
1926–   1921–

Margaret 1930– = Antony Armstrong-Jones
Earl of Snowdon 1930–

David Viscount Linley
1961–

Lady Sarah Armstrong-
Jones 1964–

The Duke of York with his elder daughter, Princess Elizabeth, just before the Yorks set out on an extended tour of Australia and New Zealand in January 1937.

Upon signing the Declaration of Abdication Act on 11 December 1936, King Edward VIII said of his brother and successor: "He has one matchless blessing, enjoyed by so many of you and not bestowed on me, a happy home with his wife and children."

Bertie, the Duke of York, was indeed fortunate with his choice of bride, although at the time of his marriage no one knew quite how important his choice would be to the nation.

His marriage to Lady Elizabeth Bowes-Lyon had taken place in Westminster Abbey on 26 April 1923. He was a shy twenty-eight-year-old with a stammer, and had always been over-shadowed by his elder brother Edward and his sister Mary. Lady Elizabeth was a friend of Princess Mary and had been a bridesmaid at her wedding in 1922. She liked Bertie but was initially reluctant to take on the responsibilities of becoming a member of the royal family, and she gently declined his first proposal of marriage. She was only twenty-three years old and the increasingly irascible King admired both her honesty and her beauty. He said to Bertie, "You'll be a lucky fellow if she accepts you". She did, however, accept him when he proposed again, and the engagement was announced in *The Times*. The flood of letters of congratulation prompted her to say to a friend, with slightly grim humour: "That cat is now completely out of the bag and there is no possibility of stuffing him back."

The King gave the young couple White Lodge in Richmond Park as their first home, but they soon found this to be too far away from London for their many engagements. They moved into a succession of town houses, either lent or taken furnished, and their first child was born at 17 Bruton Street, the town house of the Duchess's parents, the Earl and Countess of Strathmore, on 21 April 1926.

Their baby daughter was third in line to the throne. The Duke wrote to his father to ask his consent to their choice of names. "Elizabeth and I have been thinking over names for our little girl & we should like to call her Elizabeth Alexandra Mary. I hope you will approve of these names, & I am sure there will be no muddle over two Elizabeths in the family. We are so anxious for her first name to be Elizabeth as it is such a nice name & there has been no one of that name in your family for a long time. Elizabeth of York sounds so nice too."

The Princess was christened on 29 May 1926 at the Private Chapel at Buckingham Palace. Her godparents were the King and Queen, Princess Mary, the Duke of Connaught, the Earl of Strathmore and Lady Elphinstone (sister of the Duchess of York).

Although the Yorks had no permanent home, no expense was spared on their child's comfort. A special cot was made, slung on a cream enamelled frame and trimmed with old-fashioned double curtains, golden pink satin under a paler shade of patterned net, edged with frills. She had a quilted cot cover, also trimmed with net, and matching pillow cases, sheets and blankets. Her first present was an ivory-handled rattle from Queen Mary. This was later handed down, in the next generation, to Prince Charles as his first toy.

The Duke and Duchess finally found a house, 145 Piccadilly, owned by the Crown Estate. It was a four-storey stone-faced terrace house, plain and solid. They were to live there for nine and a half years, although their initial occupation was delayed as the King decided that they should go to Australia to open the new Federal Parliament Buildings at Canberra, a visit that would separate them from Princess Elizabeth for six months.

The Duchess was especially sad to leave her daughter behind,

17 Bruton Street, the birth place of the future Queen.

99

The Duchess of York with her younger daughter. In her childhood she was always known as Princess Margaret Rose.

Elizabeth exercising her pony in Windsor Park, 1937. She has always been a fine horsewoman.

but she was glad to be able to entrust Elizabeth to the loving care of Clara Knight, who had been her own nanny. She was the daughter of a tenant farmer from Whitwell, Hertfordshire, and her brother farmed at St Paul's Walden Bury on the Strathmore estate. She came from a deeply religious family and was known as "Alla" (an attempt to pronounce Clara) to all her charges. When she died at Sandringham on 2 January 1946 the Duchess of York (by then Queen Elizabeth) and her daughters attended her funeral service at St Paul's Walden.

During the Yorks' absence in Australia, Alla sent coded cables to them describing Elizabeth's progress, together with long letters to await their arrival at every port. Princess Elizabeth was over fourteen months old when her parents returned.

The household at 145 Piccadilly was quite large, comprising about twenty servants living in. The staff included a butler, who was assisted by an under-butler, two footmen, an odd job man, and a steward's room boy. The housekeeper had three housemaids and the cook three kitchen maids. Alla had an under-nurse, Margaret Macdonald (known as Bobo) from Ross-shire, who shared a bedroom with Elizabeth (and is now employed as her dresser), and her sister Ruby Macdonald, the nurserymaid. The Duchess had a dresser and the Duke a valet. There was also an RAF orderly and a night-watchman, together with a Boy Scout who had lent a hand during some rebuilding and who remained with the household to serve as telephone operator.

Following the birth of Princess Margaret in 1930 the two children had a simple and orderly routine. They always saw their parents early in the morning before returning to the nursery for breakfast, and when they were a little older they were taken to join their parents after lunch.

Princess Elizabeth was first named "Lilibet" by her grandfather King George V, after her own first attempts to say her name. He was extremely fond of his granddaughters and his affection was returned. Towards the end of 1928 he nearly died, and once the crisis had passed his doctors sent him to recuperate at Bognor Regis where Princess Elizabeth visited him the following March. Queen Mary noted in her diary: "G. delighted to see her. I played . . . in the garden making sandpies."

The nurseries occupied practically the whole top floor of 145 Piccadilly, and consisted of a suite of rooms opening on to a circular gallery under a big glass dome. The night nursery had no plumbing and was equipped with a large jug and basin. Outside on the landing Princess Elizabeth kept her large collection of toy horses. She would ride them up and down the corridor and used to take off their saddles and bridles before going to bed. The day nursery was painted green and white, and furnished with old mahogany pieces and a glass-fronted cabinet in which she kept her delicate treasures, china cottages, jade and ivory figures, and glass birds and animals — a collection which had been started for her by Queen Mary. Amongst her dolls was a "pearly doll" which had been given to her at the Carnival of Costermongers in January 1928, and her other favourite possessions included a beautifully made chair from Switzerland which played a tune when sat upon, and the set of nursery china with a picture of two magpies and the inscription "Two for joy".

Before she was four the King instructed his stud groom, Owen, to teach her to ride. The King attached special importance to the ability to ride and once told his eldest son, "If you can't ride, you know, I'm afraid people will call you a duffer". Her first pony was a Shetland named Peggy, given to her by the King for Christmas 1929. At five years old she was taken out at her father's request with the Pytchley Hunt in order that she might be "blooded" but there was no kill that day. In later years she became an

Mrs Clara Knight (left) who was nanny to the Duchess of York and her daughters. Although unmarried, she was accorded the title "Mrs" as senior nurse in the royal household.

Both princesses were taken for walks in Hyde Park (centre) until the public began to recognise them. Margaret Rose is in the pram which was also used for the next generation. Elizabeth is on her new tricycle.

Princess Margaret, at her birth in 1930, was fourth in line to the throne.

The York family at the Welsh House, Royal Lodge, Windsor, which was given to Princess Elizabeth by the people of Wales on her sixth birthday.

excellent horsewoman and greatly interested in breeding race horses at the royal stud; but she never particularly enjoyed hunting.

Until the crowds began to recognise the royal carriage drawn by two bays, the princesses were taken for two-hour daily rides in Hyde Park. Later they were restricted to playing in the private grounds, Hamilton Gardens, which could be entered through French windows from the house. The gardens contained a small lake and led on to Hyde Park. Weekends were always spent at Royal Lodge, Windsor Park, which had 15 acres of garden and was given to the Yorks by King George in 1931.

It is here that the famous model house stands. It was given to Princess Elizabeth on her sixth birthday by the people of Wales. It is fifteen feet high and is in the style of a traditional Welsh cottage, thatched, and with walls painted cream. It contains six rooms including a bathroom with hot and cold water. "Y Bwthyn Bach" (The Little House) is inscribed over the door. The Welsh Terrier Association, knowing how fond she was of dogs, presented her with a puppy named Ianto to make her home complete. A miniature garden was made for it, with a central sun dial and plots edged with box hedges. Elizabeth had always enjoyed playing "house", and for her third birthday the Countess of Airlie, lady-in-waiting to Queen Mary, gave her a dustpan and brush. She was amused to see the "resultant passion for housework" in the nursery.

Alla was very scrupulous about tidiness, and Princess Elizabeth became rather obsessively neat and tidy. Always her clothes were precisely arranged and folded before going to bed and she collected the ribbons from chocolate boxes carefully rolled up and stored with pieces of coloured paper. Nothing was ever wasted.

In October 1931 Princess Elizabeth was a bridesmaid at the wedding of Lady May Cambridge to Captain Henry Abel Smith, at Balcombe, Sussex. She wore a white fur wrap and was presented with a white lily from the church for her good behaviour. Another bridesmaid was Lady Alice Montagu-Douglas-Scott, who, four years later, was to marry Elizabeth's uncle, Prince Henry. Elizabeth was again a bridesmaid at the marriage of her uncle Prince George to Princess Marina in 1934.

The proud new owner of the Welsh House.

There was always intense public interest in both princesses, especially Elizabeth. *Time* magazine put her on their cover as a fashion setter when she was only three years old. She was celebrated in wax at Madame Tussaud's, a six-cent stamp in Newfoundland bore her likeness, and in Antarctica a territory was named Princess Elizabeth Land. The attention lavished upon Elizabeth alarmed her mother, who wrote to Queen Mary: "It almost frightens me that the people should love her so much. I suppose it is a good thing, and I only hope she will be worthy of it, poor little darling."

Queen Mary was keen on taking her granddaughters around London for "instructive amusements". Their visits included the Tower and the various museums. Both she and the King were extremely interested in the education of the two girls. The Duchess of York was anxious that Elizabeth should be given a chance to grow up in an uncomplicated way, and suggested that she should be sent to a boarding school, but the King was quite adamant that she should be educated privately at home. His principal reason was that, as she was third in line to the throne (and the Prince of Wales still showed no signs of marrying), she

The princesses with their governess, Marion Crawford, on their first outing on the London underground.

would require a special syllabus which a conventional school could not provide.

The government agreed that she should be educated at home. The Duchess of York chose the governess, Marion Crawford, aged 22, who had been with the family of the Earl of Eldon, and subsequently with her sister, Countess Granville. She was from Dunfermline, had an honours degree from Edinburgh University, and a passion for long country walks. She was an excellent choice and was much loved by her charges until, after leaving the royal family, she published a number of books and articles about the princesses which were regarded as a betrayal of trust.

Under this new regime Elizabeth's day would follow this pattern: wake at 7.30 for breakfast alone with Miss Crawford (or "Crawfie" as she was soon called); 9.00–9.15 with parents; 9.15–11.00 lessons; 11.00 break spent either walking or riding; 11.45 more lessons followed by lunch, which she would take with her parents if they were at home. Afternoons, piano playing, dancing or drawing. Tea was in the schoolroom at 4.45, and then she and Margaret would spend an hour with their mother in her sitting-room. This was a favourite time for the two sisters, as their mother would read a story and then they would act out the story and the various characters. Bedtime was at 6.45.

The schoolroom was an upstairs room at home which was exclusively used for this purpose. Miss Crawford, who began her employment with the family when Elizabeth was six, found that her pupil had already been taught to read by her mother, and had also begun to speak a little French. She was also interested in history and English literature and, later, in geography (she had a travelling rug with a map of Australia embroidered upon one side). Mathematics were beyond her, and she showed neither interest nor aptitude.

In time she spent longer hours on her lessons, and Crawfie gave way to Mr (later Sir) Henry Marten, who became chief tutor. He was formerly Vice-Provost of Eton, and gave Elizabeth special instruction in the British Constitution and economic principles. A later French teacher was Mlle Georgina Guérin, whose mother had taught the Duchess of York, and she was followed by the Vicomtesse de Bellaiges as senior French teacher.

Piano practice at Windsor, June 1940.

During World War II the princesses were moved for safety to Windsor Castle. This picture shows them helping the war effort knitting amongst the spring daffodils in 1940.

She instituted "French only" lunch sessions.

The schoolroom hours were strictly adhered to and took priority over all but the most important functions. Elizabeth got on well with Crawfie, though she did occasionally display a certain imperiousness. Once when she had been rude to her she was "sent to Coventry" as a punishment. Next morning the Princess greeted her governess with her customary "good morning" and was met with a stony silence. On the third attempt to elicit a reply she added pointedly, "It's royalty speaking".

Canon Crawley, of St George's Chapel, Windsor, supervised Elizabeth's religious instruction, and Queen Mary gave both granddaughters lessons in deportment. Lady Airlie remembered: "Even at the end of her life she used to look back with happiness to the afternoons when Miss Crawford brought the two little girls to tea at Marlborough House."

The Duchess of York taught her daughters how to address various high-ranking persons, and made the lessons into a game. She would sweep into the room and act the part of the Archbishop of Canterbury, Queen Mary or the Prime Minister and the girls had to make the appropriate greeting. A friend said, "she was so good at getting on with her children. She made fun out of nothing — and she taught them by example".

This peaceful existence was shattered for ever upon the death of the King on 20 January 1936, and the subsequent abdication of King Edward VIII in December of the same year. The family

A characteristic photograph of Princess Elizabeth in the garden at 145 Piccadilly. Later that year the family moved into Buckingham Palace.

moved from Piccadilly into Buckingham Palace and the Duke of York ascended the throne as King George VI. The momentous day of her father's coronation was recorded by Princess Elizabeth in her exercise book. "At 5 o'clock in the morning I was woken up by the band of the Royal Marines striking up just outside my window. I lept out of bed and so did Bobo. We put on dressing gowns and shoes and Bobo made me put on an eiderdown as it was so cold and we crouched in the window looking on to a cold, misty morning." Princess Margaret was less thrilled about the whole thing. She said that she had only just learnt to write the "of York" part of her name, and now she was just Princess Margaret "of nothing". She was, however, quite excited about her uncle's abdication, and asked Elizabeth whether this would mean that his head would be cut off.

At the coronation, on 12 May 1937, the two princesses walked into the Abbey on either side of their aunt the Princess Royal to their places in the royal gallery over the tomb of Anne of Cleves, each wearing a long train of purple velvet. When the Archbishop set the crown of the Queen Consort upon their mother's head each of them put on the coronet of a King's daughter, a gold circlet ornamented with crosses formy and fleur-de-lis designed by their father. Princess Margaret behaved well during the long ceremony except for occasionally whirring through her prayer book rather loudly. Then they drove back in the procession to the Palace where they appeared on the balcony.

The two princesses were now obliged to participate more often in court life. A lady-in-waiting recalled: "My first waiting was at an afternoon party at Buckingham Palace. . . . I remember Princess Elizabeth and Princess Margaret were present — real little girls. It was all rather alarming and strange for them, but the Princesses were quite composed, if a little shy."

When the blitz hit London the young family was swept off to Windsor, along with Alla, Bobo and the corgis. During an air raid they would retreat to the dungeons; although there were brighter times too, such as a Christmas pantomime in 1941 in which the princesses performed, Elizabeth as Prince Charming and Margaret as Cinderella.

Elizabeth, at the outbreak of the war, was seen as the repre-

The unforgettable moment of kingship: the coronation of George VI on 12 May 1937.

Mabell, Countess of Airlie, with Princess Elizabeth at Glamis. Lady Airlie was a lady of the bedchamber to Queen Mary, and was grandmother to the Hon Angus Ogilvy, who later married Princess Alexandra.

sentative of the young generation, and on 12 October 1940 she made her celebrated broadcast to the children of the Empire. "We children at home are full of cheerfulness and courage. We are trying to do all we can to help our gallant sailors, soldiers and airmen, and we are trying, too, to bear the danger and sadness of war. We know, every one of us, that in the end all will be well." This was heard in South Africa by Sarah Gertrude Millin, the writer, who noted in her diary: "It was perfectly done. If there are still queens in the world a generation hence, this child will be a good queen."

Princess Margaret is four years and four months younger than her sister, and was raised in much the same way. Their parents did their best to prevent rivalry between the two, although inevitably there were clashes, especially as Elizabeth, though a very confident child, was essentially introverted, whereas Margaret was pure extrovert.

Margaret had irrepressible high spirits which delighted her father, and he also loved her wicked mimicry and practical jokes — a family trait. Elizabeth and Margaret were often dressed the same and were given more or less the same attention from their parents, but their characters were clearly quite different.

The last royal child to be born in Scotland was Charles I (not counting his younger brother, Robert, who only lived four months) until the birth of Princess Margaret. She was born at 9.22 pm on 21 August 1930, on a dark and stormy night, at Glamis Castle, Angus. This is the Strathmores' huge and forbidding home in Scotland, and the place where it is alleged King Duncan was murdered by Macbeth (there is good authority that Duncan's grandfather, King Malcolm, was killed there in 1034). She was christened Margaret Rose in the Private Chapel at Buckingham Palace by Cosmo Lang, Archbishop of Canterbury, on 20 October, her godparents being the Prince of Wales, Princess Victoria (daughter of Edward VII), Princess Ingrid of Sweden, Countess Granville and the Hon David Bowes-Lyon (brother and sister of the Duchess of York).

A love of music has often been associated with the royal family, but it must have come as a surprise to the Duke of York when he heard his younger daughter hum the *Merry Widow* waltz at the age of nine months! (Some say that Princess Margaret was taught it at a later age by her mother as a birthday present for the Duke.) In any event, Margaret was musically gifted. It was also quickly noted that she hated to be left out of things (quite naturally), rather like Princess Anne with Prince Charles. On one occasion, when Elizabeth had won a life-saving swimming certificate, Margaret, not to be outdone, and in the middle of a Palace garden party, lured a corgi into the lake and then dived in to rescue it.

She had a vivid imagination and invented a creature called "the Pinkle-Ponkle" which flew about the sky, and would, when he came to earth, eat worm sandwiches and caterpillar jam. Another fantasy person was "cousin Halifax" whom she would blame when admonished for being naughty. She rather enjoyed monsters, and when shown a picture of a horrible dragon merely said, "What a darling Loch Ness Monster!"

Like Elizabeth, she was educated by Crawfie, though she did not receive tuition from Sir Henry Marten. Sometimes there were trips into London, to the Military Tournament, the Horse Show, or the Aldershot Tattoo. They also attended the King's Silver Jubilee celebrations, and a special treat was a ride on the London underground with Crawfie in 1939. They were not allowed to travel by bus, however, until 1946.

Princess Elizabeth with the Challenge Cup swimming team at the Bath Club, 1939.

Elizabeth often liked Margaret to be included in her games, and when a Palace Girl Guide pack was formed she asked for Margaret to join as a Brownie. Margaret loved to make people laugh, and Crawfie reported: "Every night I would watch the same performance. From the tent that housed Margaret there would burst forth storms of giggles. The Guides officer would appear, say a few words, and retreat. The ensuing silence would reign for a minute or two, then a fresh outburst probably meant Margaret was giving her companions an imitation of the Guides officer's lecture." Sometimes her mimicry was aimed at her sister, and she would quite cruelly mock Elizabeth's "a place for everything and everything in its place" attitude. On the other hand, she had considerable charm, and her father boasted that "she could persuade the pearl to come out of an oyster".

Princess Margaret's marriage to Antony Armstrong-Jones (later created Earl of Snowdon) took place in Westminster Abbey

Lady Sarah Armstrong-Jones and Viscount Linley with their parents Princess Margaret and the Earl of Snowdon.

The schoolroom at Buckingham Palace.

on 6 May 1960 and was dissolved by divorce in May 1978. The nanny she employed was Miss Sumner, who is now retired and lives in a small flat in Elephant and Castle owned by the Duchy of Cornwall. She has two children. The eldest, David Albert Charles, Viscount Linley, was born at Clarence House on 3 November 1961, and christened in the Music Room at Buckingham Palace on 19 December. His godparents are the Queen, Lady Elizabeth Cavendish, Lord Plunket, Lord Rupert Nevill, and the Rev Simon Phipps (now Bishop of Lincoln).

Lord Linley had a rather scattered education. First he went to two pre-preparatory schools, Gibbs in Kensington (where his cousin Prince Edward was later sent), then to Ashdown House, Forest Row, Sussex, where he boarded for four years. This was followed by Millbrook School, near Abingdon, where he prepared for the entrance exam to his father's old school, Eton. It eventually became clear that he would not pass this, and he had no wish to go there in any case. It was decided that he should go instead to Bedales, a progressive, co-educational school in Hampshire.

This was a happy choice as he made many friends there and was able to spend much of his time working at carpentry, at which he excels. He is now doing a two-year course for craftsmen run by John Makepeace, at Parnham House in Dorset, and is likely to make a career in design.

His sister, Lady Sarah Frances Elizabeth Armstrong-Jones, was born on 1 May 1964. She was christened at the private chapel at Buckingham Palace by the Dean of Westminster, Dr Eric Abbott. Her godparents are Mrs Eric Penn, Mrs Jane Stevens, Marigold Bridgeman, the Earl of Westmorland, and Anthony Barton. Lady Sarah won great admiration as the chief bridesmaid at the marriage of her cousin the Prince of Wales to Lady Diana Spencer in 1981, and was previously bridesmaid to both Princess Anne in 1973 and to the Princess of Wales' sister, Lady Sarah Spencer, in 1980.

Like her brother she was educated at Bedales School, where she is now in her final year. She is especially close to the Prince of Wales, and was captured in a delightful photograph by the Earl of Lichfield skipping about with the Prince on the moor at Balmoral on his twenty-fourth birthday.

Lady Elizabeth Bowes-Lyon (now Queen Elizabeth the Queen Mother) with her younger brother, the Hon David Bowes-Lyon, at their family home, Glamis Castle in Scotland.

A fine portrait by Lord Snowdon of his two children. Both went on to Bedales School, and Lady Sarah begins a course at Camberwell School of Art in September 1982.

Elizabeth II's Children

Right from the start, the Queen decided
that Prince Andrew would not suffer from
the excessive press exposure that had
made some aspects of Prince Charles's
early life quite unbearable.

*Prince Philip and Princess
Elizabeth with Charles and the
infant Anne.*

The Royal Family at Balmoral.

Edward in 1973 (opp. page, left) preparing to snap his sister, at hunter trials. He is reported to be an excellent photographer, and has his own dark-room at Buckingham Palace.

Charles and Edward under starter's orders (right).

Prince Charles with his favourite musical instrument and his favourite brother, Prince Edward. Charles is the musical one in the family.

King George VI and Queen Elizabeth celebrate Charles's third birthday in the Bow Room at Buckingham Palace. Princess Elizabeth and Prince Philip were away on a tour of North America. The King died only seven weeks after the photograph was taken.

The Queen Mother smiling proudly at her new grandson, Prince Andrew, on her 60th birthday at Clarence House. Photographs of both Andrew and Edward as babies are rare, as the Queen wished to keep her younger children out of the public eye.

A typical family photograph of the Queen and Prince Philip with Andrew, Edward and dogs, at Balmoral.

The Queen with members of her family on the balcony of Buckingham Palace. The younger members are Marina Ogilvy, Prince Edward, the Earl of St Andrews, Lord Linley and Lady Sarah Armstrong-Jones.

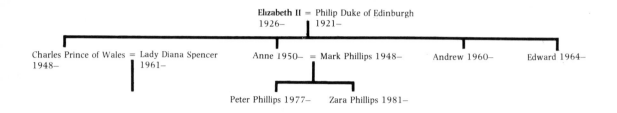

Biographers of the royal family do not agree on the precise moment when the Queen first met her future husband, although it is certain that they both attended the marriage of Prince George, Duke of Kent, to Princess Marina of Greece, who was a first cousin to Prince Philip, in 1934.

The significant meeting, however, took place on 22 July 1939, when George VI, accompanied by his daughters, took a nostalgic tour around the Royal Naval College, Dartmouth, with his second cousin, Lord Mountbatten. Lord Mountbatten's nephew had recently joined Dartmouth as a young cadet, and to him was assigned the task of entertaining the two princesses. This young cadet was, of course, Prince Philip of Greece.

Crawfie, the Princess's governess, later recalled: "He was goodlooking, though rather off hand in manner. He said, 'How do you do,' to Lilibet and for a while they knelt side by side playing with trains. He soon got bored with that. We had ginger crackers and lemonade in which he joined, and then he said, 'Let's go to the tennis courts and have some real fun jumping the nets'." At that time Philip was eighteen and Elizabeth was thirteen. The tennis courts eventually lead to the front row of a Christmas pantomime, Aladdin, at Windsor in 1943, in which Princess

Elizabeth performed; and, finally, to the aisle of Westminster Abbey, where they were married on 20 November 1947.

Prince Charles was welcomed into the world with an enthusiasm which has never since abated. He was born at Buckingham Palace at 9.14 pm on Sunday, 14 November 1948 — the first royal birth there since that of Princess Patricia of Connaught in 1886. The news was announced with the triumphant pealing of the bells of St Paul's and Westminster Abbey, while enthusiastic crowds gathered outside the palace and the fountains ran with blue water. Prince Philip was swiftly summoned by the King's Private Secretary, Sir Alan Lascelles, from a game of squash he had been playing with Lieutenant Commander Michael Parker — an excellent way of releasing tension! — and greeted Princess Elizabeth with champagne, roses and carnations. After all the anxiety following the abdication of Edward VIII the succession to the throne was at last assured.

This new generation saw several immediate changes in the traditions surrounding the Royal Family. One particularly antique custom now abandoned was the presence of the Home Secretary at all royal births. This dated from the troubled times of the Stuart kings when it was rumoured that at the confinement of James II's wife Mary of Modena a midwife had smuggled in an imposter child in a warming-pan. One imagines that both the Princess and the then Home Secretary, James Chuter-Ede, were quite happy to put their trust in Sister Helen Rowe who delivered the baby.

The 7lb 6oz child slept in a cast-iron four poster cot which had been used by the King's family for over a hundred years. Clarence House had been prepared for the Princess and the Duke of Edinburgh, but for the first few months the infant and his mother stayed in a suite of rooms on the first floor of Buckingham Palace, overlooking the Mall. These rooms were soon to be used as a temporary surgery for the Princess's father, George VI, whose worsening condition had been kept a close secret from his daughter.

The child was breast-fed by his mother for the first few weeks, and soon all those who were allowed to see him began to make the usual observations. Princess Elizabeth's former governess remarked upon the resemblance to George V, but the Queen's sister, Lady

A hastily written bulletin on the gates at Buckingham Palace announcing that Prince Charles's condition is "satisfatory".

The magnificent christening cake made for Prince Charles by the students of the National Bakery School. It weighed 130 lbs and was 36 inches high. Mrs Barnes. the cook at the Edinburghs' home, Windlesham Moor, made a smaller cake for a private celebration.

Granville, reported that "the Queen says that she thinks the baby is like his mother, but the Duke is quite certain that the baby is very like himself".

Whomever it was that the Prince most resembled it is interesting to note that he was entitled to the rank of Prince only by virtue of Letters Patent being rushed through Parliament five days before his birth. An edict had been issued by King George V in 1917 which provided that the children of the *sons* of a king should have the rank of Prince or Princess but no similar provisions were made for the children of the monarch's daughter. It was only thanks to the observant Lascelles that the new Prince was not born simply Charles Mountbatten (although he may have had one of his father's courtesy titles). When the Princess ascended the throne her son automatically became Duke of Cornwall, Duke of Rothesay, Earl of Carrick, Baron Renfrew, Lord of the Isles and Great Steward of Scotland. The Queen received one ninth of the Duchy revenues each year for the Prince's maintenance and education until he reached the age of eighteen; from the age of eighteen to twenty-one she received £30,000 a year from these revenues, the rest going to the Exchequer.

Soon there were changes in the Prince's attendants. The reliable Sister Helen Rowe, having completed her duties, was replaced by two Scottish nurses, Helen Lightbody and Mabel Anderson. The former had been previously employed by the Princess's aunt, the Duchess of Gloucester, and stayed with the Royal Family until 1956. Miss Anderson, on the other hand, was selected from an advertisement she had placed in a nursing magazine. She clearly proved to be an excellent choice, and was nanny to Princess Anne, Prince Andrew and Prince Edward, and until recently was with Princess Anne's family.

On 15 December the Prince was christened Charles Philip Arthur George in the Music Room at Buckingham Palace. The silver gilt font designed by Prince Albert was brought from Windsor and the child was baptised with holy water from the river Jordan, a tradition which dates from the Crusades. He behaved with great decorum and suitably impressed his noble sponsors. His godfathers were headed by the King and consisted of King Haakon of Norway, the Hon David Bowes-Lyon (brother of the Queen), and

Prince George of Greece (Prince Philip's last surviving paternal uncle). His godmothers were the Queen, Princess Margaret, the Dowager Marchioness of Milford Haven (grandmother of Prince Philip) and Lady Brabourne, daughter of Earl Mountbatten of Burma.

Even in these exalted surroundings there was a note of post-war austerity. Mrs Barnes, who was the Edinburghs' cook at their rented country house, Windlesham Moor, Berkshire, and who also attended the christening, was obliged to limit the amount of sugar in the cake. The baby was also issued with a ration card and a milk allowance, while Prince Philip looked out some of his old baby clothes with which to supplement his son's wardrobe. Five days after the christening Dr Jacob Snowman came to the Palace to circumcise the Prince.

In July 1949 Princess Elizabeth and her husband moved into Clarence House where a blue and white nursery overlooking a

Princess Elizabeth and Prince Philip with Charles and Anne in the gardens at Clarence House, 1951. They were to move into Buckingham Palace the following year.

The christening of Prince Charles. Standing, left to right, are Lady Brabourne, the Duke of Edinburgh, the King, the Hon David Bowes-Lyon, the Earl of Athlone and Princess Margaret. Seated are Queen Mary, Princess Elizabeth and her baby, and the Dowager Marchioness of Milford Haven. The infant Prince is wearing the robe Queen Victoria had made for the christening of her children.

Charles and Anne keeping in touch!

walled garden had been prepared. Nanny Anderson took her royal charge for rides in St James's Park in a huge old pram that Princess Elizabeth had particularly asked to have brought from Royal Lodge, Windsor. In these very early days there were no fears for the Prince's safety, but by the age of three the level of public interest in the royal children had risen to such a degree that they had to be taken for walks further afield in Putney Heath or Richmond Park, and always accompanied by a detective.

By the time of his first birthday Prince Charles's father had resumed his career in the Royal Navy and was stationed on HMS *Chequers* at Malta. The Princess also had to spend more time on her duties and it was inevitable that there would be frequent absences of one or both parents, so it must have pleased the Duke of Edinburgh and Princess Elizabeth to be able to tell their son that he would soon be presented with a brother or sister.

Not long after the birth of Princess Anne nursery life followed a fairly rigid routine. The children were roused at 7.00 am, dressed and fed in the nursery, and then taken by Mrs Lightbody at 9.00 to play with their mother for half an hour, followed by a morning walk and lunch at 1.00 (boiled chicken and rice being Charles's favourite dish). The afternoons were usually spent in the garden or in St James's with nanny and the Duke's terrier, Shandy. There were also occasional visits to great-grandmother Queen Mary at Marlborough House. Although Queen Mary no longer demanded quite the same degree of formality from her family, she still expected the young Prince to bow before he kissed her cheek, and Princess Anne to attempt to curtsey. They would always be back at Clarence House for tea at 4.30 pm, after which there would be games with their mother for half an hour before she bathed them and tucked them up in bed. This was the part of the day that Princess Elizabeth would always make special time for.

There is a well known photograph of Prince Charles with his grandfather the King. This was on the occasion of his third birthday which was spent at Buckingham Palace as his parents were away touring North America and Canada, and is the only recollection the Prince now has of his grandfather. The photograph remains a particular favourite of the Queen's.

Charles in a jaunty hat, out for a walk in St James's Park with Nurse Anderson.

King George VI died quite suddenly in the early hours of 6 February 1952. The move back to Buckingham Palace was a sorrowful one. The new Queen was anxious that her children should feel as far as possible at home in their comparatively strange surroundings, so the nursery was carefully re-created along the lines of the one at Clarence House: the box of soldiers, the cuckoo clock and the ten-feet-high mock Tudor dolls' house were all carefully installed. The nursery consisted of six rooms overlooking Constitution Hill. When lessons began one of them was adapted into a schoolroom, although the emphasis was still on comfort and safety rather than discipline. Later a small kitchen was fitted up, to the relief of the nursery page who's job it had been to bring the meals all the way from the Palace kitchens – a distance of several hundred yards across the width of the Palace, and up and down several flights of stairs.

The Queen chose to break with royal tradition when she decided that her son and daughter were not to make the customary bow and curtsey to her. This was in line with her wish that the Prince should simply be addressed as "Charles" by the Palace staff. There were, however, other changes which must certainly have given the young Prince a clue about his future life. These changes included the addition of his own footman, an eighteen-year-old Palace servant named Richard Brown and — more ominously — a private detective named Sergeant Kelly.

Having set the date for her coronation (2 June 1953), the Queen announced that her son would not be required to swear the oath of allegiance, although it was arranged that he would witness this tremendous occasion incognito (that is, not in ducal robes, but in a beautiful white satin suit). He was duly escorted by Mrs Lightbody in a plain car to the Abbey, where he slipped in through a side-door past the Poet's Corner and sat in the royal box between his grandmother and aunt. He left before the lengthy ceremony was completed and returned for lunch to the Palace to await the arrival of his mother and the final triumphant appearance on the balcony. If the Prince heard echoes of the

A pensive moment for the heir apparent during the coronation ceremony.

roars of the crowds as he lay in his bed that night, we might attribute to them his later remark about how he gradually became aware of his future as something that "just dawns on you slowly".

At this time Prince Charles's interests and character became more distinct. He was very fond of animals and looked after two family corgis, a hamster named Chi Chi, and two love-birds, Davy and Annie (after Davy Crockett and Annie Oakley). He was a quiet, thoughtful child with beautiful, if rather formal manners, though he could sometimes be mischievous — as a footman discovered when an ice-cube was slipped down his neck. He soon developed a deep love of the countryside, and also enjoyed being taught to ride, his first mount being a Shetland pony named Fum.

Charles hits out, at Hill House School. He was the first heir to the throne ever to be sent to school.

Prince Charles mounted. Like many of his family, he is an accomplished horseman.

Prince Charles at Royal Lodge, Windsor, the weekend retreat of the Royal Family, 1954.

In November 1953 the Queen and the Duke of Edinburgh left for the Commonwealth tour which they had abandoned in Kenya the year before on the death of George VI. As they were to be away over Christmas the Queen was careful to buy her son an especially nice present — a red, white and blue glider. They were, after all, going to be away for six months, which is a very long time for a four-year-old child. However, a surprise was in store for both Anne and Charles, for arrangements were made for them to join their parents in Tobruk the following May. So on 15 April 1954 the two children, accompanied by Mrs Lightbody, Miss Anderson and Miss Peebles, their future governess, set sail from Portsmouth on the royal yacht *Britannia*. Their first stop was Malta where they were entertained by their great-uncle Lord Mountbatten, and then they continued their journey reaching Tobruk on 2 May.

The reunion was enthusiastic. This was the first time the children had been abroad, and they were full of excited stories about their voyage. They all went on to visit Gibraltar where they were thrilled to see the Barbary apes leaping about, and where the Gibraltar Garrison presented them with a magnificent electric railway set which remains a most treasured toy in the royal nursery.

Returning home the Prince found it was time to start his lessons in greater earnest. His governess Miss Catherine Peebles — soon to be nicknamed Mispy — had previously been governess to his cousin Prince Michael of Kent. She soon realised she was dealing with a rather sensitive child. "If you raised your voice to him, he would draw back into his shell and for a time you would be able to do nothing with him." It was precisely this lack of confidence that his parents were concerned about, but they hoped that by giving him the gentle encouragement of individual attention he would gradually grow more self-assured. Thus they thought it best that Prince Charles should receive his tuition alone.

He progressed well under the care of his new governess. His reading and writing were good and he took a keen interest in history and geography. He loathed mathematics. French was added in the second year of Miss Peebles' arrival.

The Queen, who also received a solitary education, may have

feared that her son was being deprived of companions of his own age (although he did see quite a lot of his friends and relations during the holidays at Sandringham and Balmoral), and both she and the Duke of Edinburgh felt it was vital for Prince Charles to have some contact – however limited – with the lives of his future subjects. They therefore decided to make their first stand against what the historian Dermot Morrah has called the "inherited limitations of royalty". Prince Charles broke with the traditional education of the heir to the throne on 7 November 1956, when he started his first term at Hill House School, Knightsbridge, a private pre-preparatory day school, run by Colonel Townend. The press of course were there to witness this important event, although their attentions then diminished for a time. Unfortunately, press and public interest redoubled when Charles went to his second school, Cheam, at Headley on the Berkshire Downs (which his father had also attended), and the Queen's Press Secretary had to ask the editors of the national newspapers to allow the Prince to continue his education in peace. This was an unprecedented move on the Queen's part, although it was to occur again twenty-five years later, on 8 December 1981, when she appealed once more to the press to give the Princess of Wales some freedom and privacy.

Although Princess Anne was not fond of dolls, she certainly seems to be having fun with the pram. Balmoral, 1953.

The Queen and Princess Anne (opp. top right) at Peter Phillips' christening.

Captain Mark Phillips (opp. centre right) leading his son Peter on his first pony, Smokey, at Sandringham.

Charles and Anne on Coronation day (opp. left). Even at an early age Prince Charles had a helping hand for his sister.

Peter Phillips' first experience of the scene from the balcony at Buckingham Palace (opp. bottom right).

Prince Charles's later education at Gordonstoun and Geelong Grammar School followed conventional lines, and it was only at Trinity College, Cambridge, that he received his first grounding in British constitutional law in preparation for his investiture as Prince of Wales and his role as heir apparent.

Miss Anderson was in an excellent position to see quite clearly the marked differences between Prince Charles and Princess Anne. Speaking of Charles she said, "He was never as boisterous or noisy as Princess Anne. She had a much stronger, more extrovert personality. She didn't exactly push him aside, but she was certainly a more forceful child." The very different natures of the two children were already apparent, and it is tempting to infer that Princess Anne could be quite a wayward child who needed, at times, to be curbed.

Princess Anne was born on 15 August 1950 at Clarence House. The choice of the first name, Anne, was one of personal preference, although her other names, Elizabeth, Alice and Louise, all have close family associations.

The heirloom christening robe was again brought out of its cedarwood chest for the baptism of the new baby, on 21 October. The godparents were both of the child's grandmothers (Queen Elizabeth and Princess Andrew of Greece), Princess Margarita of Hohenlöhe-Langenburg (sister of Prince Philip), Lord Mountbatten of Burma and the Hon Andrew Elphinstone (Queen Elizabeth's nephew).

After the first few months, the baby girl was seen to be a bright little thing with fair curly hair, blue eyes (like most members of the Royal Family), and a pretty pink and white complexion, but these good as gold looks belied a highly spirited character. She was quite unimpressed by dolls, although her public image required her to be photographed with them, and when on one occasion she was asked the name of the doll in the pram, she replied "No name".

Princess Anne was much more interested in jig-saw puzzles, plasticine and cutting out cardboard shapes. She loved climbing trees and waving to the crowds whenever possible. Her affectionate tomboy nature was completely spontaneous, although it was mixed with a streak of stubbornness; at the time of the Coronation Princess Anne can recall screaming with fury at not

Prince Charles with the infant Prince Andrew in his cradle decorated with white lace, freesia and narcissi.

being allowed to get into the car taking her brother to the Abbey. She was always conscious of being the younger one and strove to catch up with Charles, although not necessarily to emulate him. She seldom made any attempt to curtsey to her great-grandmother Queen Mary, and when she and Charles were taken to Sandringham on the royal train Anne had to be pulled back by her brother to thank the engine driver. Similarly, Anne made the delightful discovery that simply by walking past a scarlet-clad Palace sentry she would set off a whole series of noisy movements, known as presenting arms. This would entertain her for hours, whereas Charles would take pains to avoid passing the sentries.

It was decided that unlike Prince Charles, Princess Anne would share her lessons from Miss Peebles at the Palace with two more little girls, Susan Babington-Smith and Caroline Hamilton. This was not a great success, however, for as Anne was later to admit she was inclined to be bossy. She was happier spending time with her family. Prince Philip took a special interest in teaching her to swim (by the age of six she could dive off his shoulders), and he later taught her to drive a bubble car around the private roads at Windsor.

When she was only two and a half she began riding lessons and was first taught by her mother, who started her off on a small Shetland pony. The Queen must have been amused to see at what an early age her daughter showed a distinct preference for the old rocking horse out of all the nursery toys. From the nursery windows Anne had a perfect view of the squadrons of black Household Cavalry horses as they trotted by on their way to Whitehall. She could also see the beautiful horse from the Royal Mews that appears every morning and afternoon at the Privy Purse Door, drawing a small black brougham and driven by a top-hatted coachman to collect and deliver the Royal mail.

Not surprisingly, as a change from this constant formality, Princess Anne grew up to treasure the time she could spend in old jeans and sweaters mucking out the stables or crewing for her father in a sailing dinghy. Her strong, competitive character was formed at a very early age and, in retrospect, can be seen to have worked both for and against her. Sometimes her abrupt manner has caused unnecessary offence. But with her single-minded determination she won the European Championships at the Three-Day Event at Burghley in 1971, and later that year she was voted "Sportswoman of the Year". Her marriage to Captain Mark Phillips in 1973 also captured the imagination of the public and did much to improve her rather poor public image.

Princess Anne has two children, Peter and Zara Phillips, who are of course first cousins to the new baby. Peter was born at the Lindo Wing of St Mary's Hospital, Paddington, with Mr George Pinker in attendance. He weighed 7lb 9oz and arrived at 10.46 am on 15 Nov 1977, the day after the Princess's fourth wedding anniversary. The Queen was told the good news by telephone and was ten minutes late for an investiture at the Palace. The assembled people were delighted when she proudly told them "I am a grandmother".

Peter Phillips held by his proud grandmother.

He was christened Peter Mark Andrew in the Music Room at Buckingham Palace on 22 December by the Archbishop of Canterbury, Dr Donald Coggan, and cried throughout the entire ceremony. Five generations of the royal family were there, including the 94-year-old Princess Alice, Countess of Athlone, the last surviving grandchild of Queen Victoria, and thus a great great great aunt of Peter Phillips.

Zara Anne Elizabeth Phillips was born on 15 May 1981. Her godparents are Prince Andrew, the Countess of Lichfield, Mrs Jackie Stewart, Lt Col Andrew Parker-Bowles and Hugh Thomas. Princess Anne's former nurse, Mabel Anderson, first went to their home at Gatcombe Park, Gloucestershire, to look after young Peter Phillips. She has since left and her place was taken by Pat Moss who is still there.

As for the two younger princes, Andrew and Edward, they too are quite unlike, although there are similarities to their older siblings. Andrew has something of Anne's aggressiveness, but in his case it is tempered with a great sense of humour; equally there seems to be a certain diffidence about Edward which very much reminds one of his eldest brother, although Prince Edward looks as though he has grown out of this shy stage at a much earlier age.

Prince Charles was eleven and Princess Anne nine at the time of the birth of Prince Andrew on 19 February 1960. He was the first child to be born to a reigning monarch for a hundred and three years. He was born in the Belgian suite on the ground floor of Buckingham Palace overlooking the gardens; his weight was 7lb 3oz, and he had blue eyes and light brown hair. The principal difference between this child and the elder ones was that right from the start the Queen decided that Prince Andrew would not suffer from the excessive press exposure that had made some aspects of Prince Charles's early life quite unbearable.

It was not until the registration of the baby on 22 March that the public learned of the Prince's names. He was to be called Andrew (after Prince Philip's father), Albert (which had been given to successive princes after Albert, the Prince Consort and, in particular, had been the name that George VI had been known by before he came to the throne), Christian (after Prince Philip's great grandfather, King Christian IX of Denmark) and Edward (after the Queen's great grandfather, King Edward VII). No photographs

Prince Edward dodging a snowball from Prince Andrew, at Sandringham in 1971; and (right) with his mother and sister.

134

of the christening were released, nor was the Prince seen in public for the first sixteen months of his life. The public, unused to such secrecy, began to get concerned, and eventually a rumour spread that there was "something wrong" with the new baby. To refute this Sister Helen Rowe, his nurse, gave a regular progress report, calling him "a baby full of smiles" and describing him as "simply wonderful in every respect". The first view the public had of Prince Andrew was on the balcony of Buckingham Palace following Trooping the Colour in June 1961.

These stupid and annoying rumours did not deter the Queen from her resolve to shield her son from the press. Even when he was five or six he was smuggled to and from a private gymnasium in London for physical exercise, and to an army sports ground to learn the basic rules of cricket and football. This seclusion did not seem to have any adverse effect upon the Prince; on the contrary,

Prince Charles and Lady Sarah Armstrong-Jones in an impromptu highland fling on the Prince's 24th birthday, at Balmoral.

Viscount Linley, the only son of Princess Margaret.

he became extremely outgoing and confident. Once when he was asked his age he replied, "three and a big bit".

It is well known that Prince Andrew has a fondness (and talent) for practical jokes. When he was big enough to drive a pedal car he drove it straight towards the royal corgis; he tied together the shoe laces of the guardsmen; he poured bubble bath mixture into the Windsor swimming pool; and one can imagine from the Queen's comment "Andrew was not always a little ray of sunshine" that her sense of humour was sometimes worn rather thin.

Prince Andrew also received his early education from Miss Peebles, sharing the school-room with several other young pupils. His progress was quite rapid and he soon became top monitor of this small class. It was decided that Andrew would not be sent to Cheam, where Prince Charles had been. The preparatory school chosen instead was Heatherdown, conveniently close to Windsor, and where the Hon Angus Ogilvy, who married Princess Alexandra of Kent, had spent a happy time a generation previously.

From the Prince's later career at Gordonstoun, Lakefield College, Canada, and RNC Dartmouth, it can be seen that Andrew made an easy adjustment to the demands of royal birth, and instead of resenting his position as a second son in the family he has taken advantage of any opportunity to support his brother and develop his own individual personality.

Prince Edward is still at an age when the privacy insisted upon by the Queen still secludes him. A little is known of his character, which tends to resemble his eldest brother and his mother, and shows a distinct preference for the country pursuits of birdwatching and fly-fishing. He was born on 10 March 1964, when the Queen was only a few weeks short of her thirty-eighth birthday. His early years followed the pattern of his elder brothers and sister, although by now the Queen had become more adept at dealing with her paper work and was able to spend more time with her younger children. When Prince Charles and Princess Anne were young their mother's study was strictly out of bounds, but by the time the younger two were running about the Queen was quite happy to let them play in there occasionally.

Prince Edward at Gibbs School.

The smiling six-year-old is Lady Sarah Armstrong-Jones on her birthday, with her brother Viscount Linley. Both of Princess Margaret's children have inherited an artistic talent from their father, and are the first members of the Royal Family who look likely to make a career in the arts.

The christening took place at Windsor on 2 May 1964, when the baby was given the names Edward Antony Richard Louis. The last three names were all after his godfathers: the Earl of Snowdon, Prince Richard of Gloucester and Prince Louis of Hesse. His godmothers are the Duchess of Kent, who had given birth to a daughter only a month before, and Princess George of Hanover.

Prince Edward had the companionship of three cousins, all born in the same year as himself. These were James Ogilvy, Lady Helen Windsor and Lady Sarah Armstrong-Jones; they all shared the royal schoolroom and had their riding and swimming lessons together at the Palace. Catherine Peebles, who had been governess to Prince Charles, Princess Anne and Prince Andrew, died at Buckingham Palace in September 1968, and her place was taken the following year by Lavinia Keppel, who became governess to Prince Edward. Prince Edward and James Ogilvy both went to a day school, Gibbs School in Kensington, followed by Heatherdown, and although they were later sent to different schools they have remained firm friends.

Edward was especially thrilled to be his brother's supporter at his marriage in 1981 as there has always been a close bond of friendship between the two brothers.

He is now at Gordonstoun, where academically he has surpassed his elder brothers by gaining nine "O" levels (Charles had five and Andrew six). He is now taking "A" levels in History, English and Economics with Politics, and in the holidays is embarking upon his first few public engagements.

The Royal Cousins

*The Duke and Duchess of Kent with their three children,
photographed in 1973 in the drawing room at Coppins.
Lady Helen Windsor recently attained her eighteenth
birthday.*

*The Royal Family gathered in
April 1979 for the christening of
Lord Frederick Windsor, the son
of Prince Michael of Kent (see
page 154).*

140

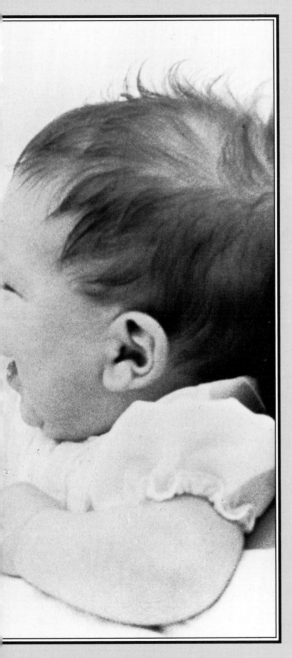

Lord Snowdon's portrait of Lord Frederick Windsor, aged three months, with his mother.

The Kents are keen and accomplished skiers. Top, left to right: the Duke, Lady Helen Windsor and Lord Nicholas Windsor, at Méribel in France in 1982. Below, left: on the steps of St George's Chapel, Windsor, after the Christmas Day service in 1976, are the Duchess of Kent and her three children, with their aunt Princess Alexandra behind. Right: the Gloucesters at the christening of their youngest child, Lady Rose Windsor, in March 1980.

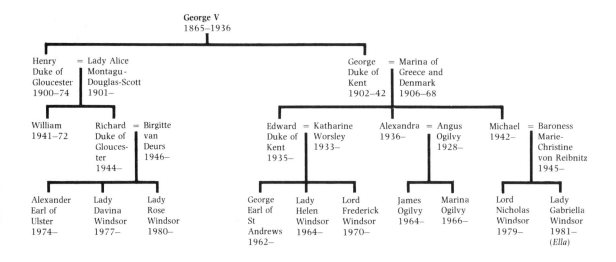

George V
1865–1936

Henry = Lady Alice
Duke of Montagu-
Gloucester Douglas-Scott
1900–74 1901–

George = Marina of
Duke of Greece and
Kent Denmark
1902–42 1906–68

William
1941–72

Richard = Birgitte
Duke of van
Glouces- Deurs
ter 1946–
1944–

Edward = Katharine
Duke of Worsley
Kent 1933–
1935–

Alexandra = Angus
1936– Ogilvy
1928–

Michael = Baroness
1942– Marie-
Christine
von Reibnitz
1945–

Alexander
Earl of
Ulster
1974–

Lady
Davina
Windsor
1977–

Lady
Rose
Windsor
1980–

George
Earl of
St
Andrews
1962–

Lady
Helen
Windsor
1964–

Lord
Frederick
Windsor
1970–

James
Ogilvy
1964–

Marina
Ogilvy
1966–

Lord
Nicholas
Windsor
1979–

Lady
Gabriella
Windsor
1981–
(*Ella*)

King George V and Queen Mary at their wedding in 1893. They are the common ancestors of the "royal cousins".

*I*n 1934 Princess Marina of Greece and Denmark set sail for Britain to marry a prince, just as her great-aunt Alexandra had done seventy-one years earlier. The warmth of the welcome she received from her new people reflected the sympathy they felt for this young girl whose family had been exiled from their native Greece, and who had suffered appalling treatment from the revolutionary government.

Marina was the youngest daughter of Prince Nicholas of Greece and Denmark, and therefore a first cousin of the present Duke of Edinburgh. Her marriage to Prince George, Duke of Kent, the youngest surviving son of George V, was extremely popular in Britain as it was a marriage for love rather than a political alliance. Moreover the Princess was quite lovely, and the Duke's pride in her was touching to see. They were married in Westminster Abbey on 29 November 1934.

Prince Edward, now the Duke of Kent, aged one, in the garden of his parents' first home, 3 Belgrave Square.

The Kents' first home was at 3 Belgrave Square, and it was here that their first child was born on 9 September 1935. Both parents were sure that it would be a boy, and even Queen Mary was sufficiently convinced to fill the toy cupboards with boyish toys. The crib was decorated with blue-for-a-boy ribbons (unlike that of Prince Charles fourteen years later which was decorated in ambiguous yellow!) Everyone's predictions were correct and soon Prince Edward George Nicholas Paul Patrick was playing in the large and sunny nursery, decorated with blue and white chintzes. In the nursery too was a beautiful and unusual rug which was made especially for Prince Edward and bore his initials. It was hand made and of a design depicting all the traditional children's nursery rhymes interwoven with colourful and charming illustrations. It is now old and faded and is carefully kept out of harm's way by Prince Michael of Kent in his apartments at Kensington Palace.

Prince Edward soon showed his preference for mechanical things: one of his first words was "car", and his favourite vehicle was a tractor. He once said to his nanny: "I love Sandringham. It's just like heaven, one tractor after another." His father was pleased that they shared an interest in machinery, and they would spend hours together messing about in the garage. By the age of 4 Edward could take his toy car to bits and reassemble it. Not surprisingly, his ambition was to be an engineer.

After the birth of Princess Alexandra Helen Elizabeth Olga Christabel on Christmas Day 1936 the family moved to the country, where the Duke had inherited Coppins, near Iver in Buckinghamshire, from his aunt, Princess Victoria (see page 66 above). It was a typical Victorian "Swiss Cottage-style" villa, unimaginative and oppressive, with a gloomy garden. The new owners had a strong aesthetic sense, and saw the potential for a lovely country house. Soon the place was full of light and beautiful furniture. It was in many ways the perfect home for a young family, standing in 130 acres including the Home Farm, where the children fed the animals, and giving them all the privacy they could wish. An outdoor gymnasium was fixed up, complete with ladders and swings, and a see-saw, slide and sand-pit.

During the early years of World War II the family was often separated. Sometimes the children stayed with their grandmother Queen Mary, who had been evacuated to stay with her niece the Duchess of Beaufort at Badminton, Gloucestershire, or else at Windsor or York Cottage, Sandringham. Once they went as far afield as the Devon coast. Later, a protective steel roof was constructed over the day nursery at Coppins, and the children could play there safely even during an air-raid.

It was at Coppins that Prince Michael was born on 4 July 1942. He was christened Michael George Charles Franklin. The last name was in honour of President Roosevelt, who was a close friend of the Duke, and one of the baby's godfathers; although at the height of the war, hardly surprisingly, he was unable to attend the christening.

The Kents were an affectionate family, and their friends were touched by the evident love and attention both parents gave their children. In her diary the Baroness de Stoeckl observed the Duke and his new son:

Prince George, Duke of Kent, with his wife and children, Edward and Alexandra, at Coppins in July 1941. The Duke is wearing the uniform of a group captain in the RAF. He was tragically killed in a flying accident on active service the following year.

> Every evening instead of sitting late as usual, he leaves the table shortly after 10 o'clock and carries his youngest son to the nursery and lays him on his cot and stands watching and watching. Nanny told me that each night as he lays his son in his cot she discreetly leaves the room, but she can hear the Duke talking softly to him. Perhaps he is unconsciously preparing him for the future.

146

The Duke was tragically killed in a flying accident on active service, only seven weeks after the birth of his son.

The person who received this dreadful news was the faithful Miss Fox. She had been Princess Marina's governess, and had come back to live in Britain. Although she was not employed as nanny to the children, she was always invited to come to see each new child and to give advice. Princess Marina was utterly devastated by the death of her husband, and it was primarily her responsibility to her children that gave her the strength to come through. The tranquil security of Coppins must have been of great comfort to her at this time, for although the Duke had provided a trust for his childrens' education, the allowance from the Civil List was severely reduced.

The children were raised quietly at Coppins. Their royal position seems not to have inhibited them at all: Edward and Alexandra attended a local private day-school and they made friends in the village — the twin sons of the local doctor being especially close. Alexandra entered the village gymkhana on her pony, Trusty, and the boys would occasionally help with the milk round on their bicycles before school. Their holidays were spent either at Birkhall on the Balmoral estate, where Princess Marina would fly-fish, or at St Margaret's Bay in Kent.

Edward (who became Duke of Kent upon his father's death) was sent to a preparatory school named Ludgrove, near Wokingham, founded by Charles I. This was followed by Eton College, for which he had been put down at the age of four months. He also had a tutor in the holidays, Giles St Aubyn, who was a master at Eton. Alexandra set a precedent by being the first girl in the Royal Family to go to a boarding school. She was sent at the age of eleven to Heathfield, where her best subjects were English, French, History and Art. She was later sent to France where her formal ecucation was rounded off.

Princess Marina showed herself to be an excellent judge of character when she employed Catherine Peebles as Michael's governess. Miss Peebles was a spirited Scotswoman full of charm and commonsense, and could deal effectively with Alexandra and Michael's occasional stubbornness as well as Edward's temper. Alexandra nicknamed her "Bambie", but the name that finally stuck was "Mispy", and that was how she was always known by Prince Charles and her later royal pupils. Michael showed a keen interest in geography, and was encouraged by Queen Mary who sent him a special set of pictorial maps. Both he and Alexandra were musical, and when still a small boy he played the tambourine in the school percussion band. He amused his uncle King George VI by saying: "We've got a pin-cushion band at our school, and I'm playing the tangerine in it!" His childhood ambition, however, was to join the fire brigade. He was sent to Sunningdale preparatory school, followed by Eton.

George, Earl of St Andrews, on his fifth birthday, at Coppins. He is the elder son of the Duke and Duchess of Kent.

Summing up, a friend of Princess Marina said: "She gave them a solid, sensible education. No extravagance, no nonsense and no false values. She is devoted but very firm." Following the marriage of her elder son, the Duke of Kent, to Miss Katharine Worsley in 1961, Princess Marina moved into apartments at Kensington Palace, where she died in 1968.

Of the present Duke's children, the elder two were born at Coppins. The eldest child is George Philip Nicholas, Earl of St Andrews, born on 26 June 1962. He weighed 6lb 4oz and, like most of the House of Windsor, had blue eyes and fair hair. This time the edict of George V needed no amendment and this baby was the first descendant in the male line from George V not to bear the title of Prince.

The christening was performed in the Music Room at Buckingham Palace by the Archbishop of Canterbury on 14 September. The child was named after his grandfather the late Duke, and his godparents are Prince Philip, Princess Alexandra, Lady Serena Lumley and Oliver Worsley, brother of the Duchess. Like Princess Marina, the Duchess chose a Scotswoman as nanny. The young woman she employed was Mary McPherson, who had formerly been a nursemaid to the Balmoral factor.

As the Duke was a serving army officer, the small baby had a far-travelled infancy. He was taken with his parents to the independence celebrations in Uganda in 1962, and this was followed by a year in Hong Kong during which they returned to Britain to attend the marriage of Princess Alexandra to the Hon Angus Ogilvy in April 1963. They left George in the care of Miss McPherson and a Chinese amah who, on their return, described the crawling

Lady Helen Windsor, only daughter of the Duke and Duchess of Kent, on her fifth birthday. In 1980 she went to Gordonstoun, where she is now studying for her "A" levels.

baby as "the little one with winged knees!"

Then came a year in Germany, after which the family finally returned to Coppins in the autumn of 1965, bringing with them their baby daughter, Lady Helen Marina Lucy, who was born on 28 April 1964. This was *the* year of royal births, for no less than four occurred in as many months. First was Princess Alexandra's son, James Ogilvy, in February; then the Queen gave birth to Prince Edward in March; Lady Helen was next in April, and finally Lady Sarah Armstrong-Jones was born to Princess Margaret in May. There had not been such a succession of royal births since 1818 following the death of Princess Charlotte, when four of her elderly uncles were obliged to put away their mistresses and beget a legitimate heir to the throne, the eventual result being Queen Victoria.

Lady Helen was named after Princess Marina's mother. She was christened on 12 May, ten days after Prince Edward — the first royal christenings to be held in the private chapel at Windsor since that of Prince Richard of Gloucester twenty years before. The Dean of Windsor, the Very Rev Robert Woods, officiated, and her godparents are Princess Margaret, Mrs David Butler, the Hon Angus Ogilvy and Sir Philip Hay.

At $3\frac{1}{2}$ the Earl of St Andrews was twice a page boy, first in January 1966 at the wedding of Miss Fiona Bowes-Lyon to Joseph Goodhart, and again in the same month at the marriage of Lord Herbert (now Earl of Pembroke) to Miss Claire Pelly. At the first wedding he burst into tears; but by the end of the year he was sufficiently composed to win a Sooty glove puppet for singing "Away in a Manger" at a children's Christmas concert.

He quickly settled into the routine at the local day-school, Eton End, Datchet, where the children were taught music and movement, culminating in an end-of-term play in which he was a gnome. At home there were riding lessons on his pony, Lucifer. Other interests were plane-spotting and model-making. He was later sent to Heatherdown, like Prince Andrew and Prince Edward, and subsequently delighted his parents by winning a King's Scholarship to Eton. This has always been a highly competitive scholarship, and when Lord St Andrews took the exam there were some 76 candidates competing for 15 places. He came eighth, and was top in French. Although he suffered an unexpected set-back when he failed two of his three "A" level exams, he is still regarded as the most academic of the royal cousins, and, at the time of writing, has retaken his "A" levels and is awaiting his Oxford and Cambridge entrance results.

Lady Helen also went to Eton End, then on to St Paul's preparatory school, London, followed by St Mary's, Wantage, where she took her "O" levels. She is currently at Gordonstoun taking "A" levels.

The Kent's third child, Lord Nicholas Windsor, was born on 25 July 1970 while his father was still stationed in Cyprus, commanding a squadron of the Royal Scots Greys. The birth took place at King's College Hospital, Denmark Hill, and the Duchess telephoned her husband from there to give him the news. Like his sister, Lord Nicholas was christened in the private chapel at Windsor. Prince Charles is among his godparents.

Lord Nicholas Windsor, younger son of the Duke and Duchess of Kent, at nine days.

The family moved to Anmer Hall on the Sandringham estate in 1973. This attractive house sits in a ten-acre park and has four bedrooms and a nursery wing. Miss McPherson left the family some time ago; her youngest charge, Lord Nicholas, is at present at school at Sussex House, London. He has inherited an interest in music and, at the age of 10, became the first member of the royal family to perform in a Covent Garden opera – he had a walk-on part in Mozart's *Magic Flute*. At home he has his own dog, a black spaniel named Clover.

Princess Alexandra and her husband, Angus Ogilvy, live at Thatched House Lodge, which is leased from the Crown Estates. This early eighteenth-century house is the only one within the royal park of Richmond still in private hands. It has three acres of grounds and is surrounded by tall bushes to keep the deer (and the public) at bay.

It was here that her two children were born; first, James Robert Bruce on 29 February 1964 (leap year), then Marina Victoria Alexandra on 31 July 1966. Their nanny, Olive Rattle, is now retired, although she still comes to help out in the school holidays. James's early schooling took place at Buckingham Palace with Prince Edward, and this was followed by Gibbs School, Heatherdown and Eton, where his father had also been. There he

Princess Alexandra and Angus Ogilvy with their children, James and Marina, at Thatched House Lodge.

passed "O" level exams in thirteen subjects and "A" levels in three; and he has now left Eton to attend a London "crammer" in order to improve his "A" level grades and hopes to obtain a place at Oxford University. His interests include architecture, art and photography, and he is a good pianist.

Marina Ogilvy started off by being pony-mad like Princess Anne. Her first pony was an old blanket draped over the low branch of a tree. Now she shows more interest in music, and is an accomplished pianist. Dance is another of her interests — she once danced in a children's ballet at the Theatre Royal, Drury Lane. Like her cousin Lady Helen, she went to St Mary's, Wantage. In June 1981 she stood sponsor to her cousin Lady Ella Windsor.

Nanny Rattle, a traditional nanny of the most loved kind, has carefully kept all the baby clothes used by Marina and her brother, as well as all their old toys, so that they may be passed on to Marina when she has a family of her own.

Angus Ogilvy refers to his family as the "mini-royals", for just as their home is hidden from the glare of London, so are their lives, as members of the royal family, relatively sheltered.

Princess Michael of Kent leaving hospital after the birth of her daughter Lady Ella on 23 April 1981. With her is her elder child, Lord Frederick Windsor.

Prince Michael of Kent (opp. top left) showing a precocious talent for steering with one hand. He later graduated from dodgems to bobsleigh racing, and won the British bobsleigh championship in 1972.

Prince Michael of Kent (opp. top right) on holiday at Bognor Regis, Sussex. The five-year-old Prince was a page at the marriage of his cousin Princess Elizabeth to Lieutenant Philip Mountbatten in 1947.

James Ogilvy (opp. bottom left) pushing a barrow of sand on his third birthday, is being teased by his cousin the Earl of St Andrews.

Prince Henry, Duke of Gloucester (opp. bottom right), on horseback. King George considered it essential that his sons should be taught to ride.

Prince Michael of Kent too is still allowed to live fairly privately, although he attracted a lot of publicity when in June 1978 he married Baroness Marie-Christine von Reibnitz, who is a Catholic and had previously been married to Mr Thomas Troubridge. Because of this marriage Prince Michael relinquished his place in the line of succession, although Buckingham Palace subsequently announced that his children would still be eligible to succeed to the throne.

Like both his brother and sister, and his cousins the Queen, Princess Margaret and the Duke of Gloucester, Prince Michael's first child is a son. He was born at St Mary's Hospital Paddington on 6 April 1979 and was christened Frederick Michael George David Louis at the Chapel Royal St James's Palace on 11 July. His godparents are Princess Alexandra, the Earl of St Andrews, Prince Karl-Johannes von Schwarzenberg and Mrs Andrew Geddes.

Prince and Princess Michael also have a daughter, Lady Gabriella (known as Ella) Marina Alexandra Ophelia, born on 23 April 1981. She too was christened at the Chapel Royal, on 8 June, and her godparents are King Constantine of the Hellenes, Prince Hugo Windisch-Graetz, Marina Ogilvy, the Marchioness of Douro and Lady Elizabeth Shakerley. The family spend much of their time at their country house, Nether Lypiatt Manor, near Stroud in Gloucestershire, where the children are allowed a good deal of freedom under the watchful eye of their nanny, Jean Rowcliffe, who is from Canada.

The Gloucester family precedes the Kents in the line of succession, but they are younger in age. The marriage of Henry Duke of Gloucester, third son of King George V, took place a year after that of his younger brother the Duke of Kent. His bride was Lady Alice Montagu-Douglas-Scott, third daughter of the 7th Duke of Buccleuch, and they were married at Buckingham Palace on 6 November 1935.

Their first son was not born until six years later. Queen Mary was especially delighted to have Gloucester as well as Kent grandchildren, and said quite pointedly that "Robert of Gloucester sounds so well". The names they chose, however, were William Henry Andrew Frederick. He was born on 18 December 1941 at a

nursing home run by Almira Countess of Carnarvon, which had been evacuated from Portland Place to Hadley Common, Hertfordshire. The eminent surgeon Cedric Lane Robert performed the caesarean operation. The Duke was given permission to leave his regiment to join his wife, and they spent Christmas with their baby at their home, Barnwell Manor, Peterborough, Northamptonshire.

Prince William was christened at the private chapel at Windsor on 22 February 1942. His godparents were nearly all close relatives: the King and Queen, Lord William Scott (uncle), Viscount Gort, Princess Helena Victoria and Lady Margaret Hawkins (aunt). Also present were King Haakon of Norway, King George of Greece and the Prime Minister, Winston Churchill.

Helen Lightbody arrived at Barnwell at the end of January to start her duties as nanny. She stayed with the family until Prince Richard outgrew the nursery, and she was then appointed nanny

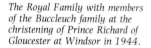

The Royal Family with members of the Buccleuch family at the christening of Prince Richard of Gloucester at Windsor in 1944.

to the Royal Family. When Mrs Lightbody was away on holiday her place was taken by Mrs Bill, who had been nanny to the Duke himself.

Prince Richard was born (also by caesarean) on 26 August 1944 at the same nursing home. When the excited Prince William was taken to see his new brother he was bitterly disappointed, and said accusingly to Mrs Lightbody: "You told me it was a little boy for me to play with and it's only a baby." Queen Mary again suggested a name for her grandchild and this time with success. He was duly christened Richard Alexander Walter George by the Archbishop of Canterbury on 20 October 1944 at the private chapel, Windsor. As we saw, it was to be the last christening there for twenty years. His godparents included the Queen (Mary), Princess Marie Louise and Field Marshal Alexander of Tunis.

On 16 December 1944 the family set sail for Australia, where the Duke was to take up his appointment as Governor-General.

An affectionate portrait of William and Richard of Gloucester.

The Duchess of Gloucester (now Princess Alice, Duchess of Gloucester) with her sons William and Richard, leaving the stables at Barnwell Manor for an early morning ride.

The Duchess of Gloucester with her elder daughter, Lady Davina Windsor, leaving Barnwell Parish Church where she was christened wearing the famous robe of Honiton lace, 1978.

The journey in war-time was extremely hazardous, and they were attacked by a German U-boat. However, they reached their destination safely having called in at Gibraltar, where William was thrilled to see the monkeys – just as Prince Charles was to do in more peaceful times.

When Prince William died tragically in a flying accident while taking part in the Goodyear Air Race, near Wolverhampton, on 28 August 1972, his mother asked Giles St Aubyn to compile a book in his memory. In this book his governess, Rosamond Ramirez, recalls her first meeting with him at the age of 5:

> I was struck by the beauty of his face and skin. The blue coat he wore accentuated the colour of his eyes which were in fact, grey rather than blue. He regarded me gravely, as children do, and then asked me a number of questions in such rapid succession that I was hardly able to keep up with them. His voice was very clear and his language I thought well-advanced for a five year old. . . . Soon after meeting William, I wrote to a friend describing my introduction to "this charming young man": his charm and dignity were already established even if at times he was exasperatingly restless and impulsive – traits which inevitably accompanied the questing and fiery elements of his nature.

There were also music and movement lessons at the Gloucesters' London home, York House, which he shared with a number of young boys and girls; and he found both the lessons and the companionship rewarding. He was later sent to a preparatory school, Wellesley House, Broadstairs, Kent, and then on to Eton and Cambridge. His death at the age of thirty was a very great loss, and he is still mourned by all who knew him.

Prince Richard later said that he was very much in his elder brother's shadow. His mother described Richard as a "very observant child and rather lazy. He only bothered to work at things that interested him". Richard, however, turned out to be more academic than his family anticipated. After his early schooling at Wellesley House and Eton he went up to Magdalene College, Cambridge, where he received a Diploma of Architecture. Subsequently he worked with the Offices Development Group of the Ministry of Public Buildings, and has illustrated with photographs *On Public View* and other books. He succeeded to the Dukedom upon the death of his father in 1974, and reluctantly gave up his career as an architect in order to spend more time on his royal duties.

In July 1972 Prince Richard married Miss Birgitte van Deurs, of Denmark, whom he met when she attended a language school in Cambridge. The birth of their first child, Alexander Patrick Gregers Richard, Earl of Ulster, was the cause of much concern as he arrived two months prematurely, and the Duchess had previously suffered a miscarriage. The baby was born on 24 October 1974 at the Lindo Wing of St Mary's Hospital, Paddington, where Mr George Pinker, the Queen's gynaecologist, performed the caesarean operation. The new-born child weighed only 4lbs and was placed in the maternity intensive care unit. The birth occurred at 1 am after a dash from Kensington Palace to the hospital; the previous day the Duchess had accompanied her husband to the House of Lords where he took his oath upon succeeding to the title of Duke of Gloucester. The Duchess quickly regained her strength and eleven days later she and her baby returned home. He was christened by the Dean of Windsor assisted by the Rector of Barnwell on 9 February 1975 at Barnwell Church. His godparents include the Prince of Wales, Princess Alexandra and the Duke of Buccleuch.

Thankfully, the Duchess had no such problems with her second child. Lady Davina Elizabeth Alice Benedikte was born on 19 November 1977, within fifty-two hours of the birth of Princess Anne's first child, Peter Phillips. She weighed 7lbs 11 oz and was christened at Barnwell by Bishop Lancelot Fleming, former Dean of Windsor.

Their youngest child, Lady Rose Victoria Birgitte Louise, was born on 1 March 1980, also at St Mary's, Paddington. She was christened in the thirteenth-century church at Barnwell on 13 July, being taken there in a pony and trap laden with flowers and driven by her proud father. Her godparents include Prince Edward and Lady Sarah Armstrong-Jones.

The Gloucesters live quietly on their estate at Barnwell, which consists of 2,500 acres and is farmed by the Duke. His mother, Princess Alice, Duchess of Gloucester, also lives there. The Duchess is assisted by a young nanny, Christine Wilkinson, who was trained at Princess Christian's College, Manchester.

The Princess of Wales

The royal wedding watched by millions throughout the world. Left: the newly married couple arrive back at Buckingham Palace. Right: the bride and her father climbing the steps of St Paul's Cathedral. Below: some of the bridesmaids, with Lady Sarah Armstrong-Jones in charge. Below right: the royal couple ride back to Buckingham Palace in an open coach, and the watching crowds get their first close look at the famous dress.

163

The Princess of Wales in formal and informal moods. Left, below: with two children at the Young England nursery school where she was working when her engagement was announced. Right: at a charity race meeting at Ascot in July 1981, in which Prince Charles took part.

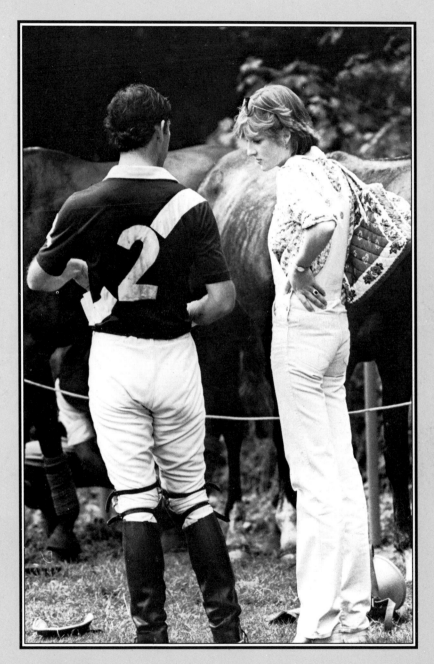

The 7th Earl Spencer, who was an equerry to the Queen from 1952 to 1954. His youngest daughter is the Princess of Wales.

*L*ooking back over the young ladies whose names the press used to associate with the Prince of Wales, there is none whose family has been so closely connected with the royal family as that of Lady Diana Spencer. It has long been the policy of the royal family to bestow personal appointments such as equerry or lady in waiting upon close friends, usually drawn from the small number of noble families which have served the Crown with discretion and loyalty from one generation to the next. Lady Diana has always been on easy terms with the royal family for precisely this reason, for her father's mother, the late Cynthia Countess Spencer, was a lady in waiting to Queen Elizabeth (now the Queen Mother); and her mother's mother, Ruth Lady Fermoy, still is a lady in waiting, also to the Queen Mother.

The Spencers have served at court since the seventeenth century, but the Fermoy associations are more recent. Their friendship with the royal family began with Lady Diana's grandfather, Maurice, 4th Lord Fermoy, who was born and raised in America but returned to Britain in 1921 and became a sporting friend to the Duke of York (later George VI.) They played ice-hockey together on the frozen lakes at Sandringham against teams made up from visiting American and Canadian troops. In 1935 George V leased Park House, on the Sandringham estate, to Lord Fermoy and his wife, and it was here that their youngest daughter, Frances, was born the following year.

In 1954, at the age of eighteen, Frances married Viscount Althorp, son and heir of the 7th Earl Spencer. Lord Althorp was an equerry to King George VI from 1950–52 and to Queen Elizabeth II from 1952–54. In 1955 Lord Fermoy died and the Queen allowed the Althorps to retain their lease of Park House. It was here that their family was raised.

The eldest is Sarah, born in 1955 (for whom Queen Elizabeth the Queen Mother is a godmother); then Jane was born in 1953 (for whom the Duke of Kent is a godfather); Diana in 1961; and lastly Charles, born in 1964 (for whom the Queen is a godmother).

All the children were born with the courtesy title of "Honourable" as the issue of a Viscount. They later became "Lady" (or, in the case of Charles, Viscount Althorp) upon the death of their grandfather the 7th Earl Spencer and the succession of their

Park House, Sandringham, Diana's childhood home, where she was "the girl next door" to Prince Charles. Park House was leased to the Fermoy family in 1935 by King George V.

An early photograph of Diana, from the Spencer family album.

father to the earldom.

Diana Frances was born on a hot summer afternoon, 1 June 1961, in the same room where her mother was born twenty-five years earlier. She was christened by the then Bishop of Norwich at Sandringham Church, where George VI and many other members of the royal family were also christened. Her god-parents are Alexander Gilmour (a first cousin to Diana's father), Lady Mary Colman (a niece of Queen Elizabeth the Queen Mother), John Floyd, Mrs Michael Pratt (daughter of a former Dean of Hereford) and Mrs William Fox.

Judith Parnell, of Kent, was nanny to the young Spencer girls, and the family was later joined in 1965 by Gertrude Allen, who had been governess to Lady Althorp. Miss Allen (known to Diana as "Ally") remembered teaching Diana to read and write and described her as "a real trier", though much more interested in outdoor games, especially swimming. At Park House they had an open-air heated pool which they shared with the younger members of the royal family during their Sandringham weekends.

This peaceful country existence was sadly interrupted by the separation of Lord and Lady Althorp in 1967. Sarah was then twelve, Jane ten, Diana six and Charles three. Lady Althorp went to live in a flat in Cadogan Place and the divorce became absolute in 1969, with custody of the children being granted to Lord Althorp. Frances, Lady Althorp, married (as his second wife) Peter Shand Kydd, and went to live in Sussex. In 1972 they

The nine-year-old Diana Spencer
enjoying a summer holiday at
Itchenor, Sussex. She was always
a "fresh air" type, and excelled
at swimming.

moved to the Isle of Seil in Scotland. The children remained at
Park House, where their father employed an *au pair* to help him
with his young family. They of course continued to visit their
mother in her new house and, later, spent school holidays with her
in Scotland. As Lord Althorp was not on good terms with his
father the children seldom stayed at Althorp House, the family
seat.

At the age of seven Diana went to her first school, Silfield, at
King's Lynn. This was followed, three years later, by a local
preparatory school, Riddlesworth Hall, near Thetford in Norfolk,
where she boarded for two years. The headmistress, Elizabeth
Ridsdale, encouraged a friendly family atmosphere. Diana fitted in
well and is remembered by Miss Ridsdale as a "kind and happy
little girl . . . she was good at games, especially swimming. . . . What
stands out in my mind is how awfully sweet she was with the
little ones".

Diana completed her two years at Riddlesworth Hall and
passed the entrance exam to West Heath School, near Sevenoaks,
Kent, where her elder sisters had also been educated. The headmistress of this school, Ruth Rudge, an Australian by origin, put
special emphasis upon character building, and combined kindness
with discipline. She particularly noted Diana's cheerful and
willing nature and her ability to get on well with everyone.
Although her academic progress never rose above a steady
average she again excelled at sport, winning various swimming
and diving prizes as well as being captain of hockey. As a young
girl Diana had been keen on riding, but she unfortunately had
an accident on her pony and broke her arm. She has not since
taken it up again.

Whilst at West Heath Diana's greatest ambition was to
become a classical ballet dancer. She had started with dancing
lessons at the age of three and a half and had continued throughout
her schooling; tap-dancing was included. Her dreams, however,
were not to be fulfilled, for she simply grew too tall (the dread of
many aspiring ballerinas). She was at West Heath for four years,
leaving in 1977 at the age of sixteen.

In 1975 Diana's grandfather, the 7th Earl Spencer, died and
her father succeeded to the title. The family left Park House and

moved into the beautiful Spencer seat, Althorp House in North-amptonshire. This was a relatively new place to the children and Lord Spencer can recall Diana's excitement at moving in. She "flew down the front staircase on a tea-tray . . . and played bears in the dark in the portrait gallery". The following year Lord Spencer married secondly, Raine, Countess of Dartmouth.

Lady Diana went in January 1978 to a finishing school in Switzerland, the Institut Alpin Videmanette at Château d'Oex, near Gstaad. Here her time was spent improving her French, and learning the arts of *haute cuisine* and skiing. Her French teacher recalled:

> "We discussed life in general and what the girls wanted to do. Lady Diana was broad-minded, but she was also very idealistic about what she wanted for herself. She knew she wanted to work with children — and then she wanted to get married and have children of her own."

Not quite a crocodile, but the children of the Young England kindergarten are safe and sound in the hands of Lady Diana.

She returned to London for the marriage in March 1978 of her sister Jane to Robert Fellowes, son of Sir William Fellowes, who was the Queen's agent at Sandringham from 1936–64. They have a daughter, Laura Jane, born in July 1980. Sarah, their eldest sister, was married in May of that year to Neil McCorquodale.

Instead of completing the one-year course in Switzerland, Diana decided to stay in London and find a job looking after young children, the work for which she had so clearly an aptitude and preference. She had no trouble in finding work as a nanny, and she particularly enjoyed caring for the two-year-old son of an American couple. In between jobs she took a three-month *cordon bleu* cookery course in Wimbledon. During this time she lived at her mother's flat in Cadogan Place, which she shared with a friend, Sophie Kimball, daughter of Marcus Kimball, the Conservative member of Parliament for Gainsborough.

In recognition of Diana's growing independence her parents bought her a three-bedroomed flat in Colherne Court, Brompton Road, where she moved in July 1979 with three friends, Carolyn Pride (a school friend from West Heath), Anne Bolton and Virginia Pitman. At this time Diana renewed her friendship with Prince Andrew, and was invited up to Balmoral in August 1979, when Prince Charles was also staying.

Since their wedding Charles and Diana have appeared frequently together in public, and undertaken numerous official engagements around Britain, although the Princess's programme was reduced as her pregnancy advanced. Whenever they are seen together their mutual love is touchingly apparent. The Princess's beautiful clothes and her exuberant sense of style and fashion have also struck every observer. She is perhaps the most photogenic of all members of the Royal Family.

In September Diana took a full time position at the Young England Kindergarten nursery school in Pimlico, run by Victoria Wilson and Kay Seth-Smith. One of the children there was Clementine Hambro, a great-granddaughter of her own distant relative, Sir Winston Churchill.

The invitation to Balmoral marks the turning point of Prince Charles's acquaintanceship with Lady Diana into friendship and deep love. Their engagement was announced by Buckingham Palace on 24 February 1981, and they were married with tremendous public acclaim in St Paul's Cathedral on 29 July, with Clementine Hambro as their youngest bridesmaid.

The Royal Baby

Less than a day after the birth, the
Princess and her son left hospital
with the proud father.
(Photo: Fincher)

*T*he Prince and Princess of Wales arrived at St. Mary's Hospital, Paddington, soon after 5 am on Monday, 21 June. She had been booked into a room twelve feet square on the top floor of the private Lindo Wing, where she was attended by the Queen's 57-year-old Surgeon Gynaecologist, Mr. George Pinker, who for nearly 20 years has been Consultant Gynaecologist and Obstetrician at the hospital.

Until the birth of the present Duke of Gloucester and his elder brother, the late Prince William, who were born at the Almira Carnarvon Nursing Home in Hertfordshire, all royal births had taken place at home. The first member of the Royal Family to be born in a hospital was Lord Nicholas Windsor, youngest child of the Duke and Duchess of Kent. He was born in 1970 at King's College Hospital, Denmark Hill, in South London. Since then all royal births have taken place at St. Mary's, Paddington, starting in 1974 with the Earl of Ulster, the eldest child of the Duke and Duchess of Gloucester, and continuing most recently with Zara, daughter of Princess Anne and Captain Mark Phillips, in May 1981. Zara was the seventh royal child to have been born at St. Mary's under the supervision of Mr. Pinker.

Mr. Pinker has stressed the importance of children being born at a hospital rather than taking risks that a birth at home may involve. Similarly he was pleased that the Princess of Wales continued to lead a full and busy life well into the later stages of her pregnancy, unlike many of her royal predecessors who have gone into almost total seclusion. Diana's last public engagement was on 18 May, when she opened the Albany Community Centre in South East London. Subsequently she was seen standing next to the Queen Mother to watch Trooping the Colour from the balcony overlooking the Horse Guards Parade on 9 June. Three days later she attended the Ascot Races, arriving in a Rolls-Royce instead of risking a bumpy ride in the traditional carriage procession, and later that day she watched Prince Charles take part in a polo match at Smith's Lawn, Windsor Great Park. This was a mere nine days before the royal birth took place on 21 June.

At 9.03 in the evening the Princess of Wales gave birth to a boy, a Prince second in line to the throne and destined one day to be King. This was the first time since the death of Edward VII in 1910, seventy-two years ago, that there have been two males, father and son, in direct succession to the throne: the future kings George V and Edward VIII.

The announcement was made in the traditional way when a notice

Prince William of Wales was christened in the Music Room at Buckingham Palace on 4 August 1982 by the Archbishop of Canterbury. His names are William Arthur Philip Louis, and his six godparents are ex-King Constantine of Greece, Lord Romsey, Sir Laurens van der Post, Princess Alexandra, the Duchess of Westminster and Lady Susan Hussey. (Photo: Camera Press/Snowdon)

Like many modern mothers, the Princess led an active life until a few days before going in to hospital. Here she is at Smith's Lawn, Windsor, where Prince Charles played polo on 12 June. (Photo: Fincher)

The announcement of the royal birth – a typed statement propped up on an elegant gilded easel in the forecourt of Buckingham Palace. (Photo: Fincher)

was posted on the gates of Buckingham Palace by Mr. Michael Timms of the Royal Household. This read: "The Princess of Wales was safely delivered of a son at 9.03 pm today. Her Royal Highness and her child are doing well." It was signed by Mr. John Batten, head of the Queen's Medical Household, Mr. Clive Roberts, the anaesthetist, Mr. David Harvey, the Princess's paediatrician, as well as Mr. Pinker. The new baby weighed 7lbs 1½oz, a good average weight, had blue eyes and fair hair, and was said to have "cried lustily". The Prince of Wales remained at the hospital throughout the day and was present at the birth.

When the news was generally released at 10.00 pm, there was tremendous cheering and applause from the large crowd which had gathered outside the hospital. The carnival spirit had stretched well beyond London but especially to Tetbury, the small Cotswold town close to Highgrove, the Prince and Princess's country home in Gloucestershire, where bunting decorated the streets, and whose townsfolk had all contributed to present the baby Prince with a silver rattle which was made in Birmingham in 1829. Prince Charles's own first present at his birth was an ivory handled rattle from his great grandmother, Queen Mary.

Looking back to the last Prince of Wales to marry when he held this title (see page 53), the future King Edward VII's bride, Princess Alexandra, was only nineteen years old – a year younger than Diana – and her first child, also a son, was born ten months after the wedding.

At the time of the announcement the Queen had just returned from a visit to the Royal Air Force base at Wittering, near Peterborough. Prince Charles telephoned his mother with the joyful news, which was also conveyed by telephone to Prince Philip, then a guest of the Master of St. John's College, Cambridge, who toasted the birth of his new grandson with a glass of brandy. Further afield, Prince Andrew was contacted on board *H.M.S. Invincible* off the Falkland Islands, and Princess Anne in America.

Prince Charles left the hospital at about 11.00 pm and was given a rapturous welcome by the throng, including the customary kiss from a blonde and the pop of champagne corks. The Prince was also the first to arrive at the hospital at about 9.00 the following morning, and was there for several hours. The constant stream of visitors comprised members of both families, including the Queen, and both of the Princess's parents. They were all delighted with the baby Prince. The proud father told the crowd, "the baby's beautiful . . . a little more human today!" He was the last to leave, a little before lunch time, giving the Princess a chance to get some well-earned rest. But later that same day, to the public's great surprise and less than twenty-four hours after the birth, the Princess and her son left the hospital and returned home to Kensington Palace by car. Mr. Pinker fully approved of this decision, saying that the Princess was in an excellent state of health.

Celebrations continued throughout the day. The King's Troop, Royal Horse Artillery, rode in full dress uniform from their barracks at St. John's Wood to Hyde Park to fire a 41-gun salute in honour of the infant Prince. At the same time the Honourable Artillery Company fired a similar number of salvoes at the Tower of London. Peals of bells rang out at Westminster Abbey from 12 noon to 1.30 pm, and a three and a half hour peal took place on the following Saturday morning. Also on 22 June St. Paul's Cathedral similarly acclaimed the birth at 5.45 after evensong. Bells of welcome also sounded from the two well-known West End churches, St. Martin-in-the-Fields and St. Clement Danes, among many others throughout the country.

Barbara Barnes, the new royal nanny, who was personally chosen for the job by the Prince and Princess of Wales. She joins a long line of rather more "starchy" predecessors.
(Photo: Press Association)

Although the Prince and Princess of Wales are determined to see more of their children than their predecessors were able to do, the person who will inevitably be closest to the new Prince during his early formative years will of course be his nanny, Barbara Barnes. Unlike Prince Charles's nannies, Miss Barnes has not had a formal training and has accumulated her knowledge from experience. Before her royal appointment, she worked for the Hon. Colin Tennant and his wife Lady Anne (a Lady-in-Waiting to Princess Margaret), looking after their three younger children. Of Miss Barnes they said: "She is exceptionally firm, with a great sense of humour. The children absolutely adore her . . . she has all the traditional virtues that you would expect to the highest degree – but she is perfectly up to date with it." Miss Barnes, who is 39, is the daughter of Mr. Billy Barnes, a former forestry worker on the estate of the Earl of Leicester. Lady Anne is the daughter of the 5th Earl.

The Prince and Princess certainly approve of Miss Barnes' modern approach. When asked by a reporter if she would be wearing the traditional nanny's uniform, the Princess replied, "Good grief, no!" – and one can imagine that Diana with her own love of children would heartily support Miss Barnes' maxim to "treat all children as individuals".

Royal Ancestry

The arms of the Prince and Princess of Wales.

ICH DIEN

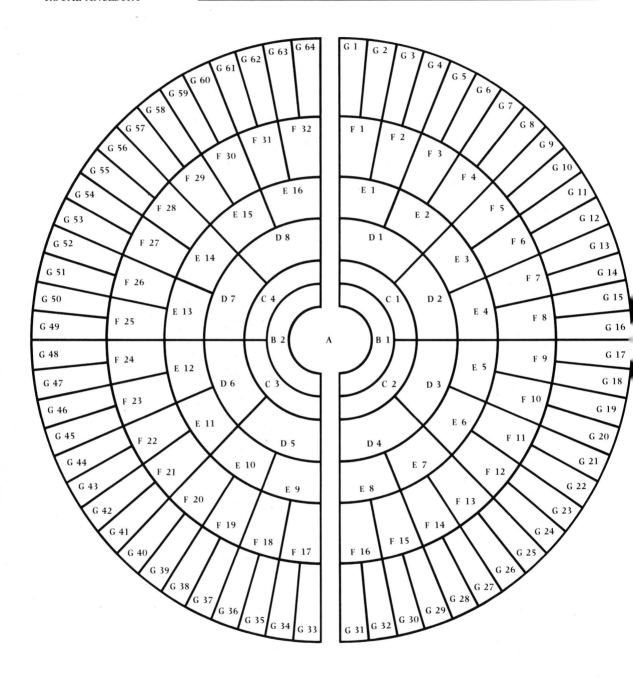

A	HRH b 1982
B 1	Charles, Prince of Wales b 1948
B 2	Lady Diana Spencer (Princess of Wales) b 1961
C 1	Prince Philip, Duke of Edinburgh b 1921
C 2	Elizabeth II b 1926
C 3	8th Earl Spencer b 1924
C 4	Hon Frances Ruth Burke-Roche b 1936
D 1	Prince Andrew of Greece d 1944
D 2	Princess Alice of Battenberg d 1967
D 3	George VI d 1952
D 4	Lady Elizabeth Bowes-Lyon (Queen Elizabeth The Queen Mother) b 1900
D 5	7th Earl Spencer d 1975
D 6	Lady Cynthia Elinor Beatrix Hamilton d 1972
D 7	4th Lord Fermoy d 1955
D 8	Ruth Sylvia Gill b 1908
E 1	King George I of Greece assass 1913
E 2	Grand Duchess Olga of Russia d 1926
E 3	Prince Louis of Battenberg, later 1st Marquess of Milford Haven d 1921
E 4	Princess Victoria of Hesse d 1950
E 5	George V d 1936
E 6	Princess Victoria Mary of Teck (Queen Mary) d 1953
E 7	14th Earl of Strathmore and Kinghorne d 1944
E 8	Nina Cecilia Cavendish-Bentinck d 1938
E 9	6th Earl Spencer d 1922
E 10	Hon Margaret Baring d 1906
E 11	3rd Duke of Abercorn d 1953
E 12	Lady Rosalind Cecilia Caroline Bingham d 1958
E 13	3rd Lord Fermoy d 1920
E 14	Frances Ellen Work d 1947
E 15	Col William Smith Gill d 1957
E 16	Ruth Littlejohn d 1964
F 1	King Christian IX of Denmark d 1906
F 2	Princess Louise of Hesse-Cassel d 1898
F 3	Grand Duke Constantine of Russia d 1892
F 4	Princess Elizabeth of Saxe-Altenburg d 1911
F 5	Prince Alexander of Hesse and the Rhine d 1888
F 6	Julia von Hauke, Princess of Battenberg d 1895
F 7	Louis IV, Grand Duke of Hesse and the Rhine d 1892
F 8	Princess Alice d 1878
F 9	Edward VII d 1910
F 10	Princess Alexandra of Denmark d 1925
F 11	Francis, Duke of Teck d 1900
F 12	Princess Mary of Cambridge d 1897
F 13	13th Earl of Strathmore and Kinghorne d 1904
F 14	Frances Smith d 1922
F 15	Rev Charles William Frederick Cavendish-Bentinck d 1865
F 16	Caroline Burnaby d 1918
F 17	4th Earl Spencer d 1857
F 18	Adelaide Horatia Elizabeth Seymour d 1877
F 19	1st Lord Revelstoke d 1897
F 20	Louisa Emily Charlotte Bulteel d 1892
F 21	2nd Duke of Abercorn d 1913
F 22	Lady Mary Anna Curzon Howe d 1929
F 23	4th Earl of Lucan d 1914
F 24	Lady Cecilia Catherine Gordon-Lennox d 1910
F 25	1st Lord Fermoy d 1874
F 26	Elizabeth Caroline Boothby d 1897
F 27	Frank Work d 1911
F 28	Ellen Wood d 1877
F 29	Alexander Ogston Gill
F 30	Barbara Smith Marr
F 31	Dr David Littlejohn d 1924
F 32	Jane Crombie d 1917
G 1	William, Duke of Schleswig-Holstein-Sonderburg-Glücksburg d 1831
G 2	Princess Louise of Hesse-Cassel d 1867
G 3	Landgrave William of Hesse-Cassel d 1867
G 4	Princess (Louise) Charlotte of Denmark d 1864
G 5	Nicholas I, Emperor of Russia d 1855
G 6	Princess Charlotte of Prussia (Empress Alexandra Feodorovna) d 1860
G 7	Joseph, Duke of Saxe-Altenburg d 1868
G 8	Duchess Amalie of Württemberg d 1848
G 9	Louis II, Grand Duke of Hesse and the Rhine d 1848
G 10	Princess Wilhelmina of Baden d 1836
G 11	Count Maurice von Hauke d 1830
G 12	Sophie la Fontaine d 1831
G 13	Prince Charles of Hesse d 1877
G 14	Princess Elizabeth of Prussia d 1885
G 15	Prince Albert of Saxe-Coburg and Gotha (Prince Consort) d 1861
G 16	Victoria d 1901
G 17	Prince Albert of Saxe-Coburg and Gotha (Prince Consort) d 1861
G 18	Victoria d 1901
G 19	King Christian IX of Denmark d 1906
G 20	Princess Louise of Hesse-Cassel d 1898
G 21	Alexander, Duke of Württemberg d 1885
G 22	Claudine Rhedey, Countess of Hohenstein d 1841
G 23	Prince Aldolphus, Duke of Cambridge d 1850
G 24	Princess Augusta of Hesse-Cassel d 1889
G 25	Thomas Lyon-Bowes, Lord Glamis d 1834
G 26	Charlotte Grimstead d 1881
G 27	Oswald Smith d 1863
G 28	Henrietta Mildred Hodgson
G 29	Lord (William) Charles Augustus Cavendish-Bentinck d 1826
G 30	Anne Wellesley d 1875
G 31	Edwyn Burnaby d 1867
G 32	Anne Caroline Salisbury d 1881
G 33	2nd Earl Spencer d 1834
G 34	Lady Lavinia Bingham d 1831
G 35	Sir Horace Beauchamp Seymour d 1856
G 36	Elizabeth Malet Palk d 1827
G 37	Henry Baring d 1848
G 38	Cecilia Anne Windham d 1874
G 39	John Crocker Bulteel d 1843
G 40	Lady Elizabeth Grey d 1880
G 41	1st Duke of Abercorn d 1885
G 42	Lady Louisa Jane Russell d 1905
G 43	1st Earl Howe d 1870
G 44	Anne Gore d 1877
G 45	Field Marshal the 3rd Earl of Lucan d 1888
G 46	Lady Anne Brudenell d 1877
G 47	5th Duke of Richmond and Lennox d 1860
G 48	Lady Caroline Paget d 1874
G 49	Edward Roche d 1855
G 50	Margaret Honoria Curtain d 1862
G 51	James Brownell Boothby d 1850
G 52	Charlotte Cunningham d 1893
G 53	John Work
G 54	Sarah Boude
G 55	John Wood d 1847
G 56	Ellen Strong d 1863
G 57	David Gill
G 58	Sarah Ogston
G 59	William Smith Marr d 1898
G 60	Helen Bean d 1852
G 61	William Littlejohn d 1888
G 62	Janet Bentley d 1848
G 63	James Crombie d 1878
G 64	Katherine Scott Forbes d 1893

*A*part from the pleasure obtained from tracing one's roots, genealogy has many practical uses. The study of family history gives useful information to the local and social historian and to the researcher in medicine. The ancestry of a future monarch is obviously of great importance, not only because of the worldwide interest in our royal family past and present, but because the character and make-up of a child is largely determined by heredity.

For the fact that the British have been so fortunate in their sovereigns, with one exception, since the accession of Queen Victoria in 1837, half the credit must rest with their spouses. When Princess Marina of Greece, who belonged to a branch of the Danish royal family, became engaged to Prince George, Duke of Kent, Queen Mary commented how pleased she was that one of this family should be marrying her son, for no one else could have handled Edward VII as well as did Queen Alexandra. The Queen's husband, Prince Philip, comes on his father's side from the same stock, and his mother was a Battenberg, sister of the great war leader, Admiral of the Fleet Earl Mountbatten of Burma.

Much of the genealogy of the Prince of Wales has been worked out by the late Gerald Paget, who after a lifetime of research published his findings when in his nineties. He traced the Prince's descent through eighteen generations, resulting in a total of about 222,400 names, many of which appeared more than once. These may be divided into three principal groups: royal and noble British forebears; a similar foreign group; and the no less interesting but untitled ancestors both at home and abroad, who are obviously more difficult to trace.

It was the custom until the sixteenth century for scions of the English and Scottish royal houses often to marry into the aristocracy. Thus the Black Prince, two of his brothers, and his nephew Henry IV all had English wives, as did Edward IV, his father and grandfather. Four of Henry VIII's six wives were Englishwomen; the second and third husbands of his elder sister, Margaret, were noble Scots; and the second husband of his younger sister Mary was a recently ennobled Suffolk man.

At a later age, a prince occasionally chose a non-royal wife — Charles I's younger son, James Duke of York, later James II, for example, married Anne Hyde, by whom he fathered two British queens. Mary II and Anne. Two princes of the House of Hanover did likewise, but this led to the passing of George III's Royal Marriages Act in 1772, giving the monarch the power of veto. Queen Victoria wisely reverted to the earlier British custom by allowing her daughter Princess Louise to marry the heir to the Duke of Argyll, and her granddaughter, then Princess Louise of Wales, to marry Lord Fife, whom she raised to a dukedom.

That marriages of members of the Royal Family with British families have multiplied since World War I owes much to the fact, obviously, that so few monarchies outside Britain have survived. Of the few remaining, some are Roman Catholics. The British Royal Family are prevented from marrying into these and still remaining in the order of succession, by the Act of Settlement passed in 1701 in order to prevent James II's Catholic son, the Old Chevalier father of Bonnie Prince Charlie, from succeeding.

This, however, was not the only reason. The rigid European policy of isolating a royal caste has reverted to the more enlightened view of freedom of choice. Queen Victoria, annoyed at the Empress of Germany's criticism of her daughter Beatrice's marriage to the morganatically born Prince Henry of Battenberg, said that she had completely ignored the more important matter of his character, and she went on to comment that "if a King chose to marry a peasant girl she would be Queen just as much as any princess".

Two great advantages of a non-royal British partner are, first, that strains of new blood are brought into the Royal Family, for most royal lines are closely inter-related; and secondly, that their descendants have a preponderance of British blood, and are therefore more easily identified with the nation. To take Queen Victoria as an example, only one of her theoretical 128 ancestors, in the seven generations prior to her, was British: this was Elizabeth, Queen of Bohemia, and her mother had been a Danish princess. (I say *theoretical* because, owing to cousin marriages, the number is drastically reduced. George I, George II and Queen Victoria herself all married first cousins.)

A large influx of British blood came into the royal house with the Queen Mother, daughter of the Earl of Strathmore, head of one of Scotland's oldest families the Lyons (recently Bowes-Lyon). Strangely enough, she had many more English ancestors than Scots, for her last six immediate forebears had chosen English wives. Tracing her ancestry to her great-great-great-great grandparents, the remainder were one-eighth Irish, and one each represented Scottish, French and American families.

As the Princess of Wales has English, Scottish, Welsh and Irish ancestors, her children inherit more British blood than any monarch since Mary Queen of Scots in 1566 gave birth in Edinburgh Castle to her only child, later James VI of Scotland and I of England.

Western European royal families are usually divided into two main groups, Protestant and Roman Catholic. Obviously most of the Prince of Wales's ancestors belonged to the former, but before the Reformation nearly all Europe, and even beyond, is represented in his geneaology. Thus we find Holy Roman Emperors, Hohenstaufen and Habsburg, the Kings of France, Carolingian and Capetian, down to Charles VI of Valois, son of Joan of Arc's Dauphin.

The first main Frankish dynasty, the Merovingians, who recently and surprisingly have been claimed to have a divine Jewish ancestry, cannot be proved as anyone's ancestors. But, as Sir Anthony Wagner points out in his *Pedigree and Progress*, when Bertha of this family wedded, and later converted to the Christian faith, Ethelbert King of Kent, it is very likely that their descendant married into the West Saxon royal house.

Sir Anthony Wagner, too, traces the Royal Family's probable descent through several Armenian dynasties, from Artaxias I, Governor of Armenia under Antiochus III of Syria, who reigned as King of Armenia from 188 to about 161 BC. The Armenians were driven out to Cilicia in Asia Minor in the eleventh century, and the Lusignans, kings of Cyprus, inherited their blood through the Lords of Jebeil (or Giblet) in

Syria. Thence through the House of Savoy this most ancient line of ancestry came to Scotland through the mother of Mary Queen of Scots. The Princess of Wales, also, can claim this ancient descent through Charlotte de la Trémoïlle, who in 1626 married the 7th Earl of Derby.

Another surprising feature in the Prince and Princess's ancestry is an inheritance of Arab blood. This has been traced through the fourth of the five wives (some say mistress) of Alfonso VI, King of Castile. She was Zayda (Morning Star), ancestress of Isabella of Castile, wife of Edmund Duke of York, the son of Edward III. Although there has been some controversy on the question whether Zayda was the daughter of Muhammad II ben Abbad, Cadi of Seville, or the widow of the Cadi's son, modern research suggests the former.

Zayda's Moslem lineage has been carried back to the Lakhmid kings of Hira in what is now Iraq, from about AD 288 to 602. This family came to Spain in 741 with Itaf, whose grandmother, Zobra, has been claimed to have been a great-granddaughter of Ali and Fatima, daughter of the Prophet Mohammed.

Another Arab descent has been traced to Musa ibn Nussir, viceroy of North Africa, who went to Morocco in 703 and died at Mecca. A descendant, Ortiga, sister of a Moorish kinglet named Alboazar, in the tenth century, was an ancestress both of the Emperor Charles V and of Pedro the Cruel, King of Castile, father of Isabella Duchess of York. When the Queen Mother's brother, David Bowes-Lyon, was in the Ministry of Information during World War II, he was shown this Arab family tree. Britain was then desperately in need of friends in the Middle East and it was arranged that copies of the genealogy should be dropped by plane to urge various tribesmen to come and help their cousin King George VI!

Two recent strains of non-royal European blood came into the Royal Family from the morganatic marriages of Queen Mary's grandfather, Prince Alexander of Württemberg, and Prince Philip's great-grandfather, Prince Alexander of Hesse. Claudine, daughter of the Count Lazzlo Rhédey, of the Transylvanian branch of that Hungarian family, met

Prince Alexander of Württemberg, a cavalry officer in the Austro-Hungarian army, at a court ball in Vienna, and in 1835 they married. Five years later she was thrown from her horse during an army manoeuvre and killed. She was buried in the family vault at Erdo Szent Gyorgy in Transylvania (now within the boundaries of Romania), and Queen Mary, who took the greatest interest in her Hungarian ancestry, erected a memorial tablet there in her memory. The Rhédey family had many noble Magyar ancestors, including the Bathory Voivodes of Transylvania; and Sir Iain Moncreiffe of that Ilk has stated that one of these was Vlad Dracul, Voivode of Wallachia, father of the original Count Dracula; and that possibly the line could be taken even further back, to Ghengis Khan.

Prince Philip's great-grandfather, Alexander of Hesse, was an officer in the Russian guards. He fell in love with the Polish Countess Julie von Hauke, one of the Tsarina's ladies in waiting. But because his sister had married the Tsarevitch, their own union was not permitted by the Tsar. So he left Russia, and entered the service of Austria, where he duly celebrated his marriage, and the Grand Duke of Hesse created Julie Countess of Battenberg.

Julie's father was Maurice, Count von Hauke, Polish War Minister and General of Artillery. Her mother Sophie, born in 1790 in Warsaw, was a daughter of Dr Leopold Lafontaine, one of the leading surgeons in Cracow, who in 1787 was appointed physician to Stanislaus II, King of Poland. The Polish forces were on Napoleon's side in the 1812 campaign, when Lafontaine was taken prisoner and died in captivity that year at Mogilev on the Dnieper.

Prince Charles descends from nearly all the British Sovereigns who had left issue, the three exceptions being Charles I and his two sons, Charles II and James II. Here the Princess of Wales is able to fill the gaps, for she can trace back to no less than five of the Merry Monarch's children by three of his mistresses, and also to Henrietta, Lady Waldegrave, James II's daughter by Arabella Churchill. The last named, as well as Charles II's daughter, Mrs Mary Sarsfield by Lucy Walter, and that king's son, the Duke of Grafton, by Barbara

Villiers, Duchess of Cleveland, are all Diana's ancestors through her grandfather, the 7th Earl Spencer. The other connections come through his wife, Lady Cynthia Hamilton.

In Scotland both Mary Queen of Scots and her husband Henry Earl of Darnley were Stuarts (originally spelt Stewart, deriving from their hereditary office of High Steward of Scotland initially before they gained the throne). The royal line goes back to the national hero of Scotland, King Robert the Bruce, and through him to the old Celtic kings. Diana, too, is of royal Stewart descent through her grandmother Lady Cynthia Hamilton, whose father, the 3rd Duke of Abercorn, descended from Mary, elder daughter of James II, King of Scots, who in 1474 married James Hamilton, Lord Hamilton. A Hamilton was heir presumptive to Mary Queen of Scots, and would have succeeded to the Scottish throne had not Mary married and given birth to a son. The Abercorn branch of the princely House of Hamilton settled in Ireland during the reign of Charles II.

Robert II's daughter Jean married, in 1376, Sir John Lyon, Chamberlain of Scotland, and brought him the Castle of Glamis, still the seat of his descendant, the Earl of Strathmore and Kinghorne. From this family the Queen Mother descends.

England has had many changes of dynasty since the West Saxon kings held sway. It is remarkable that the Prince can trace his descent from all the eleven families who ruled since King Alfred's stock kept the Danes at bay, including the hero kings, the great Alfred himself, Edward the Elder and Edmund Ironside. The last named, who fell in battle at Otford, Kent, in 1016 at the age of about 23 years, when defending his realm against the powerful Dane, King Canute, was grandfather of St Margaret of Scotland, whose daughter Matilda married the Norman, King Henry I. The Normans sneered at these two: "Leofric and Godiva", they called them.

There is also continuity with the ferocious Danish conquerors, from King Sweyn Forkbeard who defeated King Edmund's father, Ethelred the Unready. As well as fathering the mighty Canute, whose power stretched from the Atlantic to Riga on the Baltic, he had a daughter Astrid, married to Ulf Jarl, viceroy of Denmark. The sagas tell us that Ulf quarrelled with his brother-in-law Canute over a game of chess. When he took one of Canute's knights he threw it on the ground, and when it was replaced he upset the board. Next day King Canute gave orders to a house carl to have his opponent murdered. Ulf was found beside an altar with a dagger plunged into his back. One suspects that if the story be true, the quarrel was more deeply rooted than over a game. Ulf and Astrid had a son Sweyn II, who sat on the Danish throne from 1047 to 1076. From him descended in the female line, Christian I (1448–1481), the first of the present dynasty, the House of Oldenburg, to reign in Denmark. From him Prince Charles can trace his lineage in a father-to-son descent.

The Prince of Wales is as much a descendant of the valiant King Harold Godwinson, who fell at the Battle of Hastings in 1066, as he is of the conquering William of Normandy. Harold's daughter, Gytha, sought refuge at the court of King Sweyn of Denmark, and about 1070 married the Queen's first cousin, Vladimir of Novgorod, son and eventual successor of the Grand Prince of Kiev, paramount ruler of Russia. From them the line leads through the kings of Hungary to two English queens, Isabella of Valois, the "she-wolf of France", wife of Edward II, and her daughter-in-law the good Queen Philippa of Hainault, Edward III's queen. Of course Prince Charles, through his father, descends from much later rulers of Russia, the Romanovs, including Catherine the Great and Tsar Nicholas I.

Lesser known are the descents from Kings Stephen and Henry IV, first King of the House of Lancaster, whose youngest son, the Duke of Gloucester, left a bastard daughter, Antigone. This was the "good Duke Humphrey", whose library is at the Bodleian, Oxford. Antigone married Henry Grey, Count of Tancarville, and the Queen Mother can claim descent from their son, the 1st Lord Grey of Powis.

Stephen of Blois, the Conqueror's grandson, left a daughter Mary, Countess of Boulogne in her own right, who became Abbess of Romsey. She would have re-

mained there all her life had not she been abducted and forced to marry Matthew of Alsace. A triumphant entry into Boulogne was followed by the birth of two daughters. Then they separated, and she spent the last thirteen years of her life as a simple nun. From her grandson, Henry the Magnanimous, Duke of Brabant, descend the Mountbattens in the direct male line. Elizabeth Woodville, whose secret marriage to Edward IV so upset Warwick the Kingmaker, can also be traced to this duke.

The disappearance and murder of Elizabeth Woodville's two young sons, the Princes in the Tower, remains one of England's unsolved mysteries. Her daughter and heir, Elizabeth of York, united the roses by marrying the Lancastrian contender, Henry Tudor, whose defeat of Richard III in 1485, at the Battle of Bosworth Field, made him Henry VII, first king of the House of Tudor.

The Tudors were Welsh squires of Penmynydd, Anglesey, who were on the downgrade through their complicity in Owain Glyndwr's rebellion (he too is an ancestor of the Queen Mother), when they were suddenly raised to power by the marriage of Katherine of Valois, widow of Henry V, to Owen Tudor, the Keeper of her Wardrobe. The Tudors descended from Llewelyn the Great, Prince of Wales. From him the line goes back to Rhodri the Great, a ferocious opponent of the English, and to King Cadwallon, a British warrior who fell in 633 at Heavensfield near Hexham in battle against Oswald of Northumbria. Still further back, through the mists of time, one comes to the northern warriors at both ends of Hadrian's Wall: Cunedda, who migrated to Wales to defeat the Irish invaders, and Coel, the original Old King Cole, living around the last days of the Roman Empire. Historians accept both as historical characters, even if they do not agree precisely about their dates.

From the Tudors, Prince Charles descends from Henry VIII's elder sister Margaret who married James IV of Scots. In addition, through the Queen Mother, he and his wife both descend from Henry's favourite younger sister Mary, Queen of France, through her second marriage with Charles Brandon, Duke of Suffolk,

185

Washington

Spencer

who jousted with his brother-in-law Henry VIII.

Mary's granddaughter, Lady Jane Grey, whose reign for nine days was the shortest in British history, finished up on the block in the Tower. Her younger sister, Lady Catherine Grey, had an equally tragic story. Declared heir presumptive by the then current Act of Succession based on Henry VIII's will, she secretly married Edward Seymour, Earl of Hertford, son of the Protector Somerset. On Queen Elizabeth's discovery that she was married and pregnant she was thrust into the Tower; and in 1568, still in captivity, she died at Cockfield Hall, near Yoxford, Suffolk.

From Lady Catherine Grey, the Tudor line leads down to the Queen Mother, the 7th Earl Spencer and his wife, respective grandparents of the Prince and Princess. Four other royal links from the Tudors come from Mary Tudor's younger daughter Eleanor Brandon, Countess of Cumberland. These lead to Diana's grandmother, Cynthia, Lady Spencer. Thus the Princess of Wales has inherited as much legitimate blood of the Tudors as illegitimate from the Stuarts.

Many noble ancestors are shared by the royal couple. Their nearest relationship to each other is that of seventh cousin once removed, both being descended from the 3rd Duke of Devonshire. Other mutual ancestors include Queen Elizabeth's great ministers William Cecil, Lord Burghley, his son the Earl of Salisbury, Sir Francis Walsingham, and the two dictators who ran England during the reign of the boy king, Edward VI: Edward Seymour, Protector Duke of Somerset and his successor John Dudley, Duke of Northumberland, who both fell to the headsman's axe in the Tower. Northumberland's daughter, Lady Mary Sidney, was a sister of Robert Dudley, Earl of Leicester, the Queen's favourite, and mother of Mary, Countess of Pembroke, ancestress of the Prince and Princess. It was she who inspired her brother Sir Philip Sidney's *Arcadia*. Leicester's successor as the Queen's favourite, Robert Devereux, Earl of Essex, who was also beheaded, is another joint ancestor.

The raising of the *Mary Rose*, Henry VIII's flagship which sank in the Solent in 1545, is a matter of great interest to the Prince of Wales, who has more than once dived to inspect her. Not only is he a near relative of the captain, Sir George Carew, being descended from his aunt, Lady Champernowne, but the Princess is directly descended from Sir Roger Grenville, who also was drowned in the disaster.

Two families who have probably received more attention from genealogists than any other are those

Facing page, left: the Washington arms — two bars gules, in chief three mullets of the second — dating from at least 1346. They may be the origin of the Stars and Stripes. Facing page, right: Earl Spencer's arms, with the motto "God defend the right".

Althorp House in Northamptonshire, home of the Spencers since 1504.

of Shakespeare and Washington. I deal with the question of the Prince and Princess's relationship to the poet at the end of this chapter.

The Princess of Wales is the first royal descendant of the Washington family since they settled in north Lancashire in the 13th century, although it is known that their descendant George Washington and the Spencers had common ancestry in the Kitson family, and the Queen Mother and the first President are linked with the Porteus family of Virginia. Thus the royal child is a descendant of both George III and the Washingtons. Conversely, George Washington can be traced back to the Spencers.

From about 1386 the Washingtons were lords of the manor of Tewitfield in the parish of Warton, Lancashire, and Warton church contains the earliest representation of their coat of arms, the three stars and two bars, which some believe was the origin of the stars and stripes of the American flag.

Robert Washington, who paid for the rebuilding of the church tower, died in 1483, leaving two sons, John and Robert. From Robert, George Washington is ninth in direct descent. John's son Robert, doubtless called after his uncle, was Henry VIII's Serjeant of Arms, and one of his sons, Lancelot, settled in Kent.

Robert's daughter, Mary, became the first wife of John Moore of Moore's Court, Bendenden, Kent, which he sold in 1553. Both his sons by Mary Washington sought their fortune in Ireland. The younger, Sir Edward, became a forebear of the Lords Drogheda, the Ponsonbys and the Princess of Wales.

Turning to Diana's male line ancestors, the Spencers, they gained their fortune in the Midlands as rich graziers and sheep-breeders, and in 1586 it was recorded that their flock numbered 20,000. The earliest known member of the family was John Spencer of Hodnell in the parish of Wormleighton, Warwickshire, during the reign of Henry VI. His grandson, another John Spencer, was knighted and granted a coat of arms in 1504. Four years later he purchased the manors of Wormleighton in Warwickshire and Althorp in Northamptonshire, both of which he rebuilt.

The builder's grandson, another Sir John Spencer, in 1595 was given a pedigree concocted by Lee, Clarenceux King of Arms, showing a descent from a younger branch of the baronial Despenders, and on a monument erected in that year an entirely different coat of arms of the family, with due "difference", appeared. Although this remains as the coat of arms of the Dukes of Marlborough and Earl Spencer, Dr Horace

Round demolished the Despencer descent as a fabrication.

It was so accepted as a fake by the 7th Lord Spencer that he celebrated the anniversary of the original and discarded grant of arms, thus upholding a quip of the 1st Lord Spencer of Wormleighton, who was ennobled in 1603. When debating the history of English valour in the House of Lords, Lord Spencer was rudely interrupted by the Earl of Arundel, head of the Howards. "My Lord," he said, "when these things were doing, your ancestors were keeping sheep." Lord Spencer retorted, "When my ancestors were keeping sheep as you say, your ancestors were plotting treason."

Henry, 3rd Lord Spencer, who was killed fighting for the royalist cause at the first Battle of Newbury, at the age of 23 years, had recently been created Earl of Sunderland. One of his four young children, Lady Dorothy Spencer, who married Lord Halifax, is an ancestress of Prince Charles, who thus inherits Spencer blood.

When Charles, 3rd Earl of Sunderland, married for his second wife Lady Anne Churchill, daughter of the great Duke of Marlborough, he prepared the way for his son Charles eventually to inherit this dukedom and Blenheim Palace in Oxfordshire. The great Duke's widow, Sarah, however, much preferred his younger brother John, despite his once uttering a tactless remark. When his grandmother, the old Duchess, was comparing her family to a great tree, with herself at the root and all the branches flourishing about her. Jack, as he was known, commented that "the branches would flourish more when the root was underground".

Charles became the ancestor of the dukes of Marlborough and Sir Winston Churchill (in 1817 this family added the name of Churchill after Spencer). The favourite of Sarah's grandchildren was Lady Diana Spencer who, if she had been able to have her way, might have become Princess of Wales, and then history would have repeated itself! The Duchess wished her to marry Frederick, Prince of Wales, George II's son, and settled £100,000 on her, but Sir Robert Walpole

vetoed the match, and she married instead the Duke of Bedford.

John Spencer, Lady Diana's brother, inherited Althorp and as many treasures as his grandmother could leave him that were not entailed; and his son, another John, in 1765 was created Earl Spencer. The most famous Spencer, until last year, was Georgiana, Duchess of Devonshire, whose wit and charm made Devonshire House the social hub of London.

Two other ancestral relations of the Princess of Wales, as we have seen here, were Queen Victoria's ladies in waiting and in charge of the royal nursery: Lady Lyttelton, daughter of the 2nd Earl Spencer, and her successor Lady Caroline Barrington, daughter of the Reform Bill Lord Grey, whose sister Lady Elizabeth Bulteel was the 7th Earl Spencer's great-grandmother.

Diana's mother, now the Hon Mrs Shand Kydd, is a daughter of the late 4th Lord Fermoy, a descendant of an ancient Anglo-Irish family named Roche; and her grandmother, Ruth Lady Fermoy, is a member of the Gill family of Aberdeenshire.

The Roches took their name from Roch Castle in Pembrokeshire. The name means rock, and a rock appears in their crest. Adam, whose name was latinized as "de Rupe", joined in Strongbow's invasion of Ireland in the reign of Henry II, and this warlike family were recognized as Lords Fermoy by Edward IV, and as Viscounts by Elizabeth I. They forfeited their lands for supporting Charles in the Civil Wars, and when the direct line ended in 1733 it became uncertain how the peerage should descend.

The present family is a younger branch, descending from Maurice FitzEdmund Roche, Mayor of Cork, who died in 1593; and these Roches of Trebolgan, on the Co. Cork coast, received their peerage in 1856 from Queen Victoria. As Margaret Nagle, the first Lord Fermoy's great-grandmother, was doubly a first cousin of the great statesman, Edmund Burke, the name of Burke has been coupled with Roche in all recent generations.

Through Mrs Shand Kydd's grandmother, Frances Work, the American wife of the 3rd Lord Fermoy, the Princess of Wales has many interesting relations over the Atlantic. Frances' father, Frank Work, of Chillicothe, Ohio, became a millionaire in Manhattan as a stockbroker with the Vanderbilts. Other interesting connections came through Frances' mother, née Ellen Wood. The Princess of Wales is seventh cousin twice removed of Humphrey Bogart, their common ancestors having been Dorothy Parke and Joseph Morgan. Other links through Ellen Wood are Louisa May Alcott, author of *Little Women*, Nelson Rockefeller, John Pierpont Morgan, Jr, Charles Dana Gibson (creator of "the Gibson Girl", who married Irene Langhorne, sister of Nancy Lady Astor), and the wives of Caruso, Rudolph Valentino, General Patton and John Barrymore.

When the Prince of Wales bought Highgrove near Tetbury, Gloucestershire, he settled in a house built by a kinsman. This was John Paul Paul, who built Highgrove between 1796 and 1798. Richard Pitt, a

worthy Elizabethan resident of Melcombe Regis, Weymouth, Dorset, had daughters Margaret and Grace. The eldest, Margaret Pitt, married in 1583 John Bond of Lutton, Dorset, and their child, Mary, married the Rev Nicholas Paul of Berkeley, Gloucestershire. From their elder son, Onesiphorus Paul, descended a line of baronets, now extinct. The other son, Nathaniel, was a citizen and soap boiler in Bristol in the time of Charles II. His great-great-grandson built Highgrove.

Richard Pitt's fifth daughter, Grace, had married in 1596 James Ashe of Freshford, near Bradford-on-Avon, and from them came the Foleys, Harleys and Bentincks. Nine generations after Grace Pitt was Nina Cecilia Cavendish-Bentinck, wife of the 14th Earl of Strathmore and Kinghorne, parents of the Queen Mother. One never knows what will turn up in genealogy!

Above: the arms of Lord Fermoy of the Roche family, grandfather of the Princess of Wales on her mother's side. Right: Castle Roch, Pembrokeshire, from which the family name is taken.

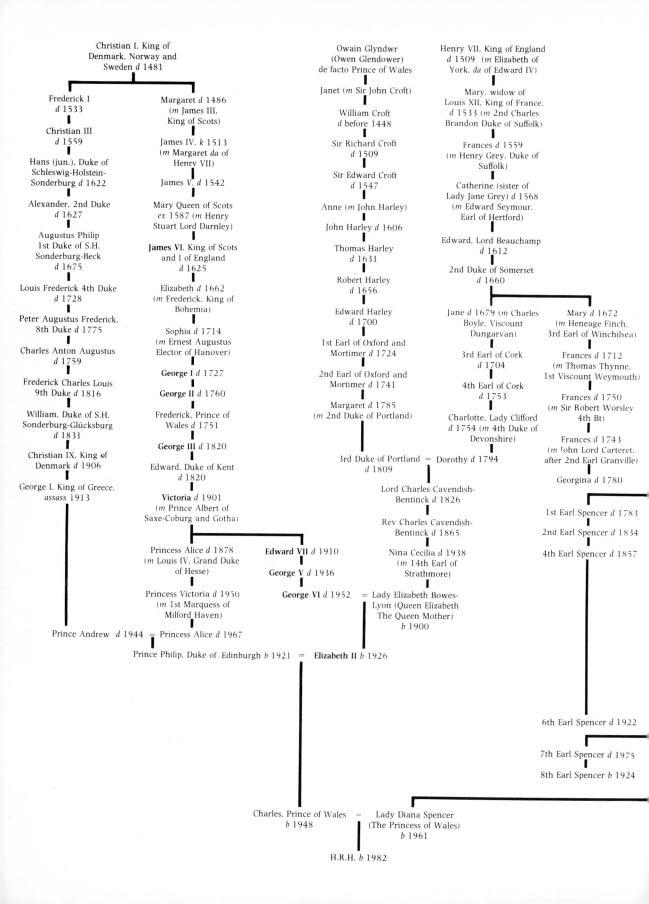

Christian I, King of
Denmark, Norway and
Sweden *d* 1481

Frederick I
d 1533

Christian III
d 1559

Hans (jun.), Duke of
Schleswig-Holstein-
Sonderburg *d* 1622

Alexander, 2nd Duke
d 1627

Augustus Philip
1st Duke of S.H.
Sonderburg-Beck
d 1675

Louis Frederick 4th Duke
d 1728

Peter Augustus Frederick,
8th Duke *d* 1775

Charles Anton Augustus
d 1759

Frederick Charles Louis
9th Duke *d* 1816

William, Duke of S.H.
Sonderburg-Glücksburg
d 1831

Christian IX, King of
Denmark *d* 1906

George I, King of Greece,
assass 1913

Margaret *d* 1486
(*m* James III,
King of Scots)

James IV, *k* 1513
(*m* Margaret *da* of
Henry VII)

James V, *d* 1542

Mary Queen of Scots
ex 1587 (*m* Henry
Stuart Lord Darnley)

James VI, King of Scots
and I of England
d 1625

Elizabeth *d* 1662
(*m* Frederick, King of
Bohemia)

Sophia *d* 1714
(*m* Ernest Augustus
Elector of Hanover)

George I *d* 1727

George II *d* 1760

Frederick, Prince of
Wales *d* 1751

George III *d* 1820

Edward, Duke of Kent
d 1820

Victoria *d* 1901
(*m* Prince Albert of
Saxe-Coburg and Gotha)

Princess Alice *d* 1878
(*m* Louis IV, Grand Duke
of Hesse)

Princess Victoria *d* 1950
(*m* 1st Marquess of
Milford Haven)

Prince Andrew *d* 1944 = Princess Alice *d* 1967

Prince Philip, Duke of Edinburgh *b* 1921 = **Elizabeth II** *b* 1926

Owain Glyndwr
(Owen Glendower)
de facto Prince of Wales

Janet (*m* Sir John Croft)

William Croft
d before 1448

Sir Richard Croft
d 1509

Sir Edward Croft
d 1547

Anne (*m* John Harley)

John Harley *d* 1606

Thomas Harley
d 1631

Robert Harley
d 1656

Edward Harley
d 1700

1st Earl of Oxford and
Mortimer *d* 1724

2nd Earl of Oxford and
Mortimer *d* 1741

Margaret *d* 1785
(*m* 2nd Duke of Portland)

3rd Duke of Portland = Dorothy *d* 1794
d 1809

Lord Charles Cavendish-
Bentinck *d* 1826

Rev Charles Cavendish-
Bentinck *d* 1865

Nina Cecilia *d* 1938
(*m* 14th Earl of
Strathmore)

Edward VII *d* 1910

George V *d* 1936

George VI *d* 1952 = Lady Elizabeth Bowes-
Lyon (Queen Elizabeth
The Queen Mother)
b 1900

Henry VII, King of England
d 1509 (*m* Elizabeth of
York, *da* of Edward IV)

Mary, widow of
Louis XII, King of France,
d 1533 (*m* 2nd Charles
Brandon Duke of Suffolk)

Frances *d* 1559
(*m* Henry Grey, Duke of
Suffolk)

Catherine (sister of
Lady Jane Grey) *d* 1568
(*m* Edward Seymour,
Earl of Hertford)

Edward, Lord Beauchamp
d 1612

2nd Duke of Somerset
d 1660

Jane *d* 1679 (*m* Charles
Boyle, Viscount
Dungarvan)

3rd Earl of Cork
d 1704

4th Earl of Cork
d 1753

Charlotte, Lady Clifford
d 1754 (*m* 4th Duke of
Devonshire)

Mary *d* 1672
(*m* Heneage Finch,
3rd Earl of Winchilsea)

Frances *d* 1712
(*m* Thomas Thynne,
1st Viscount Weymouth)

Frances *d* 1750
(*m* Sir Robert Worsley
4th Bt)

Frances *d* 1743
(*m* John Lord Carteret,
after 2nd Earl Granville)

Georgina *d* 1780

1st Earl Spencer *d* 1783

2nd Earl Spencer *d* 1834

4th Earl Spencer *d* 1857

6th Earl Spencer *d* 1922

7th Earl Spencer *d* 1975

8th Earl Spencer *b* 1924

Charles, Prince of Wales = Lady Diana Spencer
b 1948 (The Princess of Wales)
b 1961

H.R.H. *b* 1982

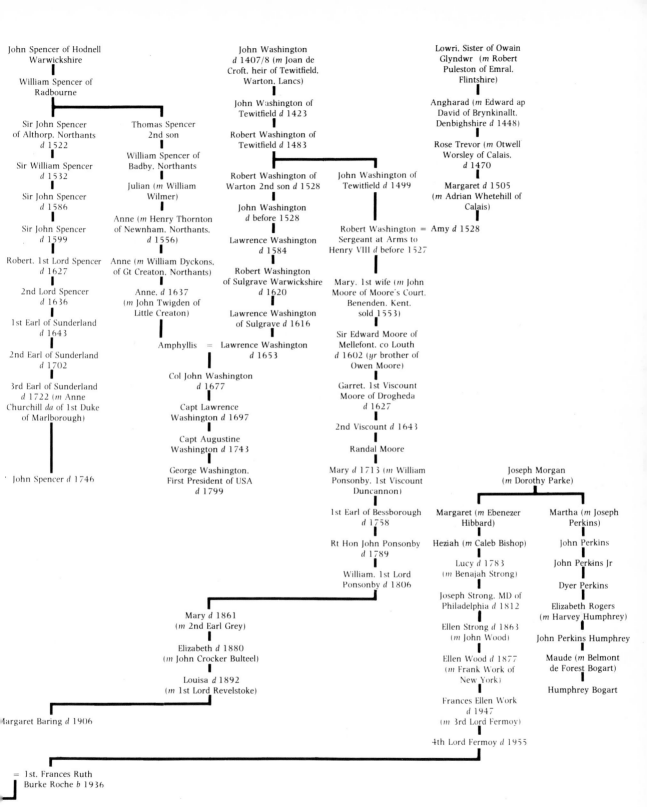

John Spencer of Hodnell Warwickshire

William Spencer of Radbourne

Sir John Spencer of Althorp. Northants d 1522

Sir William Spencer d 1532

Sir John Spencer d 1586

Sir John Spencer d 1599

Robert. 1st Lord Spencer d 1627

2nd Lord Spencer d 1636

1st Earl of Sunderland d 1643

2nd Earl of Sunderland d 1702

3rd Earl of Sunderland d 1722 (m Anne Churchill da of 1st Duke of Marlborough)

John Spencer d 1746

Thomas Spencer 2nd son

William Spencer of Badby. Northants

Julian (m William Wilmer)

Anne (m Henry Thornton of Newnham. Northants. d 1556)

Anne (m William Dyckons. of Gt Creaton. Northants)

Anne. d 1637 (m John Twigden of Little Creaton)

Amphyllis = Lawrence Washington d 1653

Col John Washington d 1677

Capt Lawrence Washington d 1697

Capt Augustine Washington d 1743

George Washington. First President of USA d 1799

John Washington d 1407/8 (m Joan de Croft, heir of Tewitfield. Warton, Lancs)

John Washington of Tewitfield d 1423

Robert Washington of Tewitfield d 1483

Robert Washington of Warton 2nd son d 1528

John Washington d before 1528

Lawrence Washington d 1584

Robert Washington of Sulgrave Warwickshire d 1620

Lawrence Washington of Sulgrave d 1616

John Washington of Tewitfield d 1499

Robert Washington = Amy d 1528 Sergeant at Arms to Henry VIII d before 1527

Mary. 1st wife (m John Moore of Moore's Court. Benenden. Kent. sold 1553)

Sir Edward Moore of Mellefont. co Louth d 1602 (yr brother of Owen Moore)

Garret. 1st Viscount Moore of Drogheda d 1627

2nd Viscount d 1643

Randal Moore

Mary d 1713 (m William Ponsonby. 1st Viscount Duncannon)

1st Earl of Bessborough d 1758

Rt Hon John Ponsonby d 1789

William. 1st Lord Ponsonby d 1806

Mary d 1861 (m 2nd Earl Grey)

Elizabeth d 1880 (m John Crocker Bulteel)

Louisa d 1892 (m 1st Lord Revelstoke)

Margaret Baring d 1906

= 1st. Frances Ruth Burke Roche b 1936

Lowri. Sister of Owain Glyndwr (m Robert Puleston of Emral. Flintshire)

Angharad (m Edward ap David of Brynkinallt. Denbighshire d 1448)

Rose Trevor (m Otwell Worsley of Calais. d 1470)

Margaret d 1505 (m Adrian Whetehill of Calais)

Joseph Morgan (m Dorothy Parke)

Margaret (m Ebenezer Hibbard)

Heziah (m Caleb Bishop)

Lucy d 1783 (m Benajah Strong)

Joseph Strong. MD of Philadelphia d 1812

Ellen Strong d 1863 (m John Wood)

Ellen Wood d 1877 (m Frank Work of New York)

Frances Ellen Work d 1947 (m 3rd Lord Fermoy)

4th Lord Fermoy d 1955

Martha (m Joseph Perkins)

John Perkins

John Perkins Jr

Dyer Perkins

Elizabeth Rogers (m Harvey Humphrey)

John Perkins Humphrey

Maude (m Belmont de Forest Bogart)

Humphrey Bogart

The Shakespeare Connection

The Princess of Wales belongs to the same male stock as did that great Englishman Sir Winston Churchill, who led his nation through the dark days of World War II to victory. There are also grounds for believing that both she and the Prince of Wales can claim kinship with that other great Englishman, William Shakespeare.

To examine the reasons for this assertion, it is necessary to delve briefly into the family history of the Ardens and their heraldry. The royal links come through Eleanor Hampden, whose family later produced Charles I's opponent John Hampden. Eleanor married Walter Arden of Park Hall, Warwickshire, and had a son Thomas. These relationships depend upon a case of identity: whether this Thomas was the same man as Thomas Arden, Shakespeare's great-grandfather.

The Ardens or Ardernes (the names were interchangeable as late as Shakespeare's day) and the Berkeleys are probably the only English families still in existence who can prove a male line descent from a powerful thegn living before the Norman Conquest. Even after 1066, Turchill of Arden held so many lands as to stand out in the Domesday Survey by occupying more than four columns.

Some of the Arden manors continued from this time until the fall of the family in 1583. Others like Sulgrave, which was later the home of the Washingtons, were acquired afterwards. Another was Park Hall at Curdworth, which Sir Henry Arden purchased in the reign of Edward III and became the chief family seat. Yet another was Langley in the Parish of Claverdon just to the north of Wilmcote, which came into the possession of Sir Henry's grandson, Robert Arden.

This Robert, MP for his county, was a staunch Yorkist during the Wars of the Roses. In this he had followed the lead of his superior lord, the all powerful Kingmaker, Richard Neville, who in 1445 had succeeded the Beauchamps as Earl of Warwick. Robert was captured, attainted and brought to the block in August 1452. His son Walter, aged two years at the time, eventually regained most of the lands, and when he died in 1502 he left a large family of six sons and four daughters. As usually happens, the lot of the younger sons did not compare with the eldest who inherited the lands, although two of them married minor heiresses.

John, the eldest, was an Esquire of the Body to King Henry VII, who later knighted him. His duties included clothing the king and serving him his pottage. Henry VII must have stayed at Park Hall, for Sir John Arden's bequests were made from the King's Chamber there.

John Arden was a colourful character, and his elopement with a neighbour, Alice Bracebridge, became part of Warwickshire folklore. John's father opposed their marriage, but Alice's father, Richard Bracebridge, proved to be their ally. He kidnapped the boy and locked them both up in a chamber at his seat of Kingsbury Park. They subsequently married, but only after a lawsuit when Richard Bracebridge was ordered to give up his best horse to John's father!

Sir John's next brother, Thomas Arden, received a fee of twenty marks a year from his father, and the remaining four had ten marks each. Of these brothers, Thomas, Martin and Robert, all survived the eldest, Sir John, who mentioned them in his will in 1526. Martin had married an heiress and lived in Oxfordshire. Robert went to court as Yeoman of the King's Chamber, and William, by then deceased, had been married into a Bedfordshire family, the Francklins, and settled at Haynes in that county. But what had happened to Thomas, the second son?

Extensive research has not yielded any information of his marriage into a landed family, and the inference is that he remained in Warwickshire. He certainly was on hand to witness his father's will in 1502.

The only Thomas Arden to be found in Warwickshire about this time was living at Wilmcote, three miles north-west of Stratford upon Avon, within the parish of Aston Cantlow, during his father's lifetime and close to his manor of Langley. Then, on 16 May 1501, Thomas acquired some more property five miles away at Snitterfield. John Mayowe transferred his land to Robert Throckmorton, Thomas Trussell of Billesley and others, including Thomas Arden of Wilmcote and his son Robert.

Some of these trustees belong to the Park Hall circle. Thomas Trussell became Sheriff of the county seven years later. The first name must have been Robert Throckmorton of Coughton, head of a leading Warwickshire family, since he preceded Trussell. A generation later, Sir George Throckmorton had in ward young Edward Arden of Park Hall, whom he proceeded to marry to his granddaughter Mary Throckmorton.

It is not known how Thomas Arden acquired his land at Wilmcote, but judging by the amount of subsidy he paid in 1523 and 1546, he was one of the principal landowners in the parish, which is quite compatible with the status of a younger son of an "armiger".

When Thomas Arden died about 1547, his son Robert lived in comparative comfort at Wilmcote, his house being adorned with "eleven painted cloths", five in the chamber adjoining the hall, two in the hall, and four in the bedrooms above, all of which were mentioned in his will. He also had solid oak furniture, candlesticks, copper pans and brass pots. These were the appurtenances of a man of substance.

Robert Arden was twice married, but only had children by his first wife (whose name is unknown), eight daughters and co-heiresses. A pattern of christian names in a family is of importance in assessing affiliation, and it should be noted that the names of all four daughters of Walter Arden of Park Hall occur among Robert's children: Joyce, Elizabeth, Margaret and Alice. Two others, Agnes and Katherine, were the names of his granddaughters, Sir John's children, which strengthens the view that Robert Arden belonged to the Park Hall family.

Robert's favourite daughter seems to have been Mary, the youngest. Not only was she his executrix, but on his death in 1556 she was bequeathed his principal estate at Wilmcote called Asbies, consisting of sixty acres. It also seems probable that he had already settled on her other property in Wilmcote, and she had a share on the reversion of his Snitterfield estate. Two farms there, with over a hundred acres, had been let to tenants, one of whom was Richard

Shakespeare. Tradition relates that Robert Arden was a devout Catholic who would not allow his Shakespeare tenants into his house, except to pay their rent.

A year after Robert Arden's death, his daughter Mary married Richard Shakespeare's son John who had previously moved into the bustling town of Stratford nearby. Their eldest son, William Shakespeare, was christened in Stratford Church on 26 April 1564.

John Shakespeare was a glover who also dealt in wool, barley and timber. He filled many offices in the borough, including bailiff (mayor), chief alderman and coroner. After he had become the Queen's chief officer, in borough records he was referred to as "Master Shakespear", and as befitted the dignity of his important status he applied to the College of Arms in 1568/9 for a grant of arms. He was a man of great extravagance, and presumably due to financial difficulties he did not then proceed beyond receiving a "pattern" or draft of arms from Robert Cook, Clarenceux King of Arms. At this time, William Shakespeare was aged four.

After a twenty-year period of impoverishment, he applied again in 1596 and was granted a coat of arms, his improved status being due to his son's successful career. Three years later, William Shakespeare purchased the imposing New Place, and that year, presumably at his behest, his father was granted an impalement of the arms of the family. In heraldry a husband's and wife's arms appear on one shield, partitioned down the centre by a vertical line. When the wife was a heraldic heiress (i.e. without brothers), these arms can later be quartered by their children. John Shakespeare died in September 1601.

The Ardens (or Ardernes) had more than one coat of arms, which is not an unusual occurrence. On John Shakespeare's first draft, the College of Arms added for his wife's impalement the coat of arms of the Park Hall family. This was of ermine, and on the fesse (a horizontal bar across the middle of the shield) was a check pattern of gold and blue. This was scratched out on the second draft, and another coat substituted: the ancient Arden coat of arms of a red shield, containing

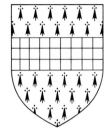

*The arms of the Park Hall
Ardens (above), "ermine
with a fesse checky gold and
azure", and (below) the more
ancient Arden arms, cross-
crosslets on a red ground, with
the red martlet "for difference".
Right: part of the draft grant of
arms to John Shakespeare of
1599, showing how the Park
Hall arms were scratched out
and the cross-crosslets
substituted.*

three cross-crosslets, with points facing downwards. On the golden chief (a horizontal bar across the top of the shield), was placed a red martlet "for difference", indicating a younger branch of the family, the Ardens of Wellingcote, as Wilmcote was then often spelt.

The first coat of arms was derived from that assigned to a mythical ancestor, Guy, Earl of Warwick, said to have lived in Anglo-Saxon days, who traditionally slew the Dun Cow, a wild boar, a green dragon and a giant. This coat was afterwards borne by the powerful Newburghs, Earls of Warwick, who also claimed descent from Guy through the Ardens. In fact King William Rufus had given them most of the Arden lands to support their new earldom.

The substituted coat of arms was based on that of the great family of Beauchamp who, after the Newburghs, also became Earls of Warwick. It is a frequent heraldic practice to derive arms from an overlord's coat. Not only were the Ardens often retainers of the Beauchamps, but the Ardens of Park Hall claimed descent, rightly or wrongly, from a junior Beauchamp heiress, Avice de Beauchamp, in the early thirteenth century. Several branches of the family, including the Ardernes of Alvanley, Cheshire, bore these arms.

Strange to say, after all this activity, Shakespeare never used the Arden quartering. By his wife Anne Hathaway, whom he married in 1582, he had a son Hamnet and two daughters, Susanna and Judith; but as Hamnet died at the age of eleven, William's hope of founding a dynasty was denied him. Shakespeare died in 1616, and was long survived by his daughters. His last descendant was his granddaughter Lady Bernard who died in 1670. There are still descendants of his sister Joan who married a Stratford hatter, William Hart, whom I discovered some years ago were living at High Wycombe.

Arguments for and against the view that Thomas Arden of Wilmcote was a younger son of Walter Arden of Park Hall have long raged, particularly in the last 120 years. There are three main criticisms, all of which can be answered.

In the nineteenth century the rigid class structure then in practice blinded many from realising the social mobility which we now know existed in the sixteenth. As Shakespeare's grandfather and great-grandfather were usually described in contemporary documents as husbandmen, it was assumed that they could not have belonged to an important landed family. This argument falls to the ground when it is realised that such descriptions were fluid. The late Oswald Barron, for instance, once referred to an esquire who was father of a husbandman. This latter term in the early fifteenth century merely meant a householder. In fact, Thomas Arden, *husbandman*, spent as much money on his subsidy at Wilmcote as did Simon Arden of Yoxall, *esquire* in 1590 when money was of less value. However, Thomas Arden was occasionally known as *gentleman*, as for example in 1525 when he served on a jury. These are the same inhibitions which have led some to believe that a clever grammar school-boy such as Shakespeare could not have had the knowledge to write his plays, and that they must have been written by Bacon, or the Earl of Oxford.

The changing of the Arden impalement to the Shakespeare coat of arms is the second criticism against a Park Hall descent. But all this implies is that in 1599 there was insufficient proof available to verify it. The first draft suggests a family tradition. Although Shakespeare's mother was then still alive, it would have been her son who attended the College of Arms. It is quite understandable that he would have been unable to prove the identity of his great-great-grandfather who died, if he were Walter, in 1502, at least thirty years before his mother's birth.

Not only is it unlikely that Shakespeare had any documents to support his claim, but his remote cousins of Park Hall had lost their lands in the debacle of 1583 (the lands were granted by the Queen to Edward Darcy). Edward Arden of Park Hall, a Roman Catholic, had gained the Earl of Leicester's emnity, and he refused to wear the Leicester livery. In 1583 his crazy son-in-law implicated him, under torture, in a threat to kill Queen Elizabeth. Leicester saw to it that Arden, though probably innocent, should be found guilty of high treason. He was executed at Smithfield, all his lands forfeited and his head set up on London Bridge. In the course of time Edward's son managed to regain some of the lands.

The late C. W. Scott-Giles in his *Shakespeare's Heraldry*, sums up the position of the Arden impalement by saying: "If the mother of Shakespeare was entitled to any arms (for although there is the strongest circumstantial evidence of her descent, it has not, as far as I know, ever been satisfactorily established), it could only have been to the so called old coat, and this was eventually assigned."

There may, however, have been a totally different explanation for the substitution: that Shakespeare himself did not wish to bear the same arms as his disgraced kinsman. We know that the unfortunate Edward's uncle, Simon Arden of Yoxall, bore the coat of cross-crosslets in 1569 and 1573 when he was Sheriff of Warwickshire, as noted by Fuller in his *Worthies* in 1662. Although this was before Edward's execution, there was probably some ill-feeling in the family. There was certainly a difference in their religion, for Simon, who moved out of Warwickshire, held a commission to enforce anti-Catholic laws in Staffordshire in 1581 and subsequently. Simon's family later reverted to the ermine and checky arms, and his descendants today represent the family.

Finally, it has been said that there were Ardens of Snitterfield before the coming there in 1501 of Thomas and Robert. A land transaction in May 1438 has been mentioned, but this refers to these same two, being a misreading of the sixteenth year of Henry VII's reign as Henry VI's.

There was an isolated instance of an Arden of Snitterfield in the mid-fifteenth century. This was a Robert, bailiff of the Earl of Warwick in that manor, who would have been a contemporary, perhaps a near relation, of Robert Arden the Yorkist. There is no evidence to conclude that he was a native of the parish, and there were no known Ardens in that district subsequently, except those of Wilmcote, as would have been likely if they had been settled there continuously. The link between the bailiff and Shakespeare's ancestors, therefore, must be regarded as being both weak and inconclusive, and all the evidence we have points to the other direction.

I agree with Mr Scott-Giles' strong presumption that the two Thomas Ardens were identical. As the case is even stronger than he realised for the reasons which I have given, I feel we may accept the poet's descent from Walter Arden of Park Hall.

The Princess of Wales descends from Barbara Hampden, a third cousin of Mary Arden, Shakespeare's mother. Barbara married secondly Sir George Paulet (sometimes spelt Pawlett) of Nether Buckland Wallop, Hampshire, and this line descends to the Spencers of Althorp through the Dowse and de Carteret families.

The Prince of Wales' descent is one generation further back. He, the Princess and Shakespeare have mutual ancestors in a Cornish knight, Sir John Whalesborough and his wife, Joan Raleigh, heiress of Nettlecombe in Somerset. There is an interesting link through her with Geoffrey Chaucer, the father of English poets. Joan's half-sister Maud Burghersh married Thomas Chaucer, the poet's son.

P.M.-S.

Sir John Whalesborough of = Joan Raleigh, heiress of
Whalesborough, Cornwall | Nettlecombe, Somerset

John Hampden, of Hampden, = Elizabeth
Bucks, *d* 1458

Thomas Hampden of Hampden, = Margaret Popham
d about 1485

Eleanor = Walter Arden of Park Hall,
Warwickshire, *d* 1502

John Hampden of Hampden, = Elizabeth Sidney
d 1496

Thomas Arden of Wilmcote, = . . .
Warwickshire, 2nd son, *d* about
1547

Sir John Hampden of Hampden, = Elizabeth Savage
d 1553

Robert Arden of Wilmcote, = 1st wife
d 1556

Barbara, co-heir, *d* 1552 = Sir George Paulet of Crondall,
Hants

Mary, co-heir, *d* 1608 = John Shakespeare of Stratford
upon Avon, *d* 1601

Sir Hampden Paulet of Nether = Anne Palmes, 2nd wife
Wallop Buckland, Hants

William Shakespeare = Anne Hathaway *d* 1623
b 1564, *d* 1616

Elizabeth Paulet, heir = Sir Francis Dowse of Broughton,
Hants, *d* 1649

Anne *d* 1644 = Sir Philip de Carteret, Seigneur of
St Ouen, Jersey and of Sark

Elizabeth *d* 1697 = Sir George Carteret of Haynes,
Beds, Lt-Gov of Jersey, a Lord
Proprietor of Carolina and Founder
of New Jersey, *d* 1680

Sir Philip Carteret, *k* in Battle of = Lady Jemima Montagu
Sole Bay 1672

George, 1st Lord Carteret, *d* 1695 = Grace Countess Granville *d* 1744

John, Earl Granville, *d* 1763 = Frances Worsley, *d* 1743

Lady Georgina Carteret, *d* 1780 = 1st, Hon John Spencer

John, 1st Earl Spencer, *d* 1783 = Georgiana Poyntz

George, 2nd Earl Spencer, *d* 1834 = Lady Lavinia Bingham

Frederick, 4th Earl Spencer, *d* 1857 = Adelaide Seymour

Charles Robert, 6th Earl Spencer = Hon Margaret Baring
d 1922

Albert Edward John, 7th Earl = Lady Cynthia Hamilton
Spencer, *d* 1975

Edward John, 8th Earl Spencer = 1st, Hon Frances Burke Roche
b 1924

Lady Diana Spencer (HRH The = HRH The Prince of Wales
Princess of Wales)

HRH the baby

Anne (*m* 2nd, Edmund Hampden = William, Lord De Moleyns, of
Stoke Poges, Bucks, *k* at Siege of
Orleans 1429

Eleanor co-heir = Robert, 3rd Lord Hungerford,
ex 1464

Sir Thomas Hungerford *ex* 1469 = Lady Anne Percy

Mary, Lady Hungerford and = Edward, 2nd Lord Hastings
de Moleyns, *d* about 1533

George, 1st Earl of Huntingdon, = Lady Anne Stafford
d 1544

Francis, 2nd Earl of Huntingdon, = Lady Catherine Pole
d 1560

George, 4th Earl of Huntingdon, = Dorothy Port
d 1604

Francis, Lord Hastings, *d* 1595 = Sarah Harington

Hon Catherine, *d* 1667 = Philip Stanhope, 1st Earl of
Chesterfield

Henry, Lord Stanhope, *d* 1634 = Hon Katherine Wotton

Philip, 2nd Earl of Chesterfield, = Lady Elizabeth Butler
d 1714

Lady Elizabeth Stanhope = John Lyon, 4th Earl of
Strathmore

Thomas, 8th Earl of Strathmore, = Jean Nicholson
d 1753

John, 9th Earl of Strathmore, = Mary Eleanor Bowes
d 1776

Thomas, 11th Earl of Strathmore, = Mary Carpenter
d 1846

Thomas, Lord Glamis, *d* 1834 = Charlotte Grimstead

Claude, 13th Earl of Strathmore, = Frances Dora Smith
d 1904

Claude, 14th Earl of Strathmore, = Nina Cecilia Cavendish-Bentinck
d 1944

Lady Elizabeth Bowes-Lyon = HM King George VI
(HM Queen Elizabeth The Queen
Mother), *b* 1900

HM Queen Elizabeth II, *b* 1926 = HRH The Prince Philip, Duke of
Edinburgh

List of Books

Airlie, Mabell, Countess of, *Thatched with Gold*, 1962

Ashdown, Dulcie M., *Royal Children*, 1979

Ashdown, Dulcie M., *Queen Victoria's Family*, 1975

Ashton, Sir George, *H.R.H. the Duke of Connaught and Strathearn*, 1929

Battiscombe, G., *Queen Alexandra*, 1969

Berkswell's *The Royal Year*, 1974 to date

Burke's *Royal Families of the World*, vol. 1, 1977

Campbell, Judith, *Anne and her Horses*, 1972

Cathcart, Helen, *The Duchess of Kent*, 1972

Clear, Celia, *Royal Children from 1840 to 1980*, 1981

Corti, Egon Caesar, Conte, *The English Empress*, 1957

De Stoeckl, Agnes, *Not all Vanity*, 1956

Donaldson, Frances, *Edward VIII*, 1974

Duff, David, *Alexandra, Princess and Queen*, 1980

Duff, David, *Elizabeth of Glamis*, 1980

Duff, David, *The Shy Princess*, 1958

Duff, David, *Hessian Tapestry*, 1967

Frankland, Noble, *Prince Henry, Duke of Gloucester*, 1980

Gore, John, *King George V, a Personal Memoir*, 1941

Halliday, F. E., *A Shakespeare Companion*, 1964

Harrison, Michael, *Clarence*, 1972

Holden, Anthony, *Charles, Prince of Wales*, 1979

Honeycombe, Gordon, *Royal Wedding*, 1981

King, Stella, *Princess Marina, her Life and Times*, 1969

Lacey, Robert, *Majesty*, 1977

Laird, Dorothy, *Queen Elizabeth The Queen Mother*, 1975

Longford, Elizabeth, *The Royal House of Windsor*, 1974

Longford, Elizabeth, *Victoria R.I.*, 1964

Magnus, Philip, *King Edward the Seventh*, 1964

Marples, Morris, *Princess in the Making, a Study of Royal Education*, 1965

Matson, John, *Dear Osborne*, 1978

Morrah, Dermot, *To be a King*, 1968

Nicolson, Harold, *King George V, His Life and Reign*, 1952

Ponsonby, Sir Frederick, *Recollections of Three Reigns*, 1951

Pope-Hennessy, James, *Queen Mary*, 1959

Roberts, Gwen, *Royal Sporting Lives*, 1971

Rowse, A. L., *Shakespeare the Man*, 1973

St. Aubyn, Giles, *The Royal George*, 1963

St. Aubyn, Giles, *William of Gloucester*, 1978

Scott-Giles, C. W., *Shakespeare's Heraldry*, 1950

Sinclair, David, *Queen and Country*, 1979

Tisdall, E. E. P., *Unpredictable Queen*, 1953

Vickers, Hugo, *Debrett's Book of the Royal Wedding*, 1981

Wagner, Anthony, "Queen Elizabeth's American Ancestry" (*Genealogists' Magazine*, vol. VIII, pp. 368–376), 1939

Wagner, Anthony, *Pedigree and Progress*, 1975

Wentworth Day, J., *H.R.H. Princess Marina, Duchess of Kent*, 1962

Wheeler-Bennett, John W., *King George VI*, 1958

Windsor, The Duke of, *A Family Album*, 1960

Windsor, The Duke of, *A King's Story*, 1951

Woodham-Smith, Cecil, *Queen Victoria, 1810–1861*, 1973

Index

Page numbers in italic refer to illustrations

A

Abbott, Dr Eric, 110
Abel Smith, Captain Henry, 103
Abercorn, Duke of, 184, 190
Abergeldie Castle, 85
Adams, Marcus, 8
Airlie, Mabell, Countess of, 87, 90, 103, 105, *108*, 200
Albert, Prince ("Bertie"), *see* George VI
Albert, Prince Consort, 9, 24, 25–6, *25*, 27, 28, 33–4, 37–8, 51, 180, 190
Albert Edward, Prince of Wales, *see* Edward VII
Albert Victor, Prince, Duke of Clarence ("Eddy"), *39*, 42, 46, 50, 53, *53*, 55, 59, *59*, *60*, 61, 63–4
Alcott, Louisa May, 189
Alexander of Battenberg, Prince, *see* Battenberg, Prince Alexander of
Alexander of Hesse, Prince, 183, 184, 190
Alexander of Württemberg, Prince, 183, 184
Alexander of Tunis, Field Marshal Earl, 157
Alexander John, Prince, *see* John, Prince, of Wales
Alexandra, Queen, 9, 24, *39*, *42*, *46*, *48*, 50–67, *51*, 55–6, *59*, *82*, 84, 182, 190
Alexandra, Princess, *11*, 14, 144, 146–8, *146*, 149, 151–2, *152*, 154, 159
Alexandra of Denmark, Princess, *see* Alexandra, Queen
Alexandra of Fife, Princess, 24, *48*, 50
Alexandra of Greece, Princess, *46*
Alfonso VI of Castile, 183
Alfred, King, 184
Alfred, Prince, Duke of Edinburgh, 6, *19*, *20*, 24, 28, *32*, 38, *38*
Alice, Princess, Duchess of Gloucester, 14, 76, 91, 103, 144, 154, *157*, 159
Alice of Albany, Princess, 24, 39, 40, *40*, 77, 133
Alice of Battenberg, Princess, *see* Battenberg, Princess Alice of
Alice of Hesse, Princess, 6, *19–20*, 24, 28, 30–31, *31*, 37, 180, 190
Alix of Hesse, Princess (later Tsarina), *20*, 24
Allen, Gertrude, 167
Althorp, Viscount, *see* Spencer, 8th Earl
Althorp, Lady, *see* Shand Kydd, Hon Mrs
Althorp House, 169, *187*
Anderson, Mabel, *13*, 122, 124, *125*, 128, 130, 133

Andrew, Prince, *11*, 14, *116*, *119*, 120, *132*, 133–6, *134*, 169, 180
Andrew of Greece, Princess, *see* Battenberg, Princess Alice of
Anmer Hill, Sandringham, 151
Anne, Princess, 9, *9*, *11*, 12, *12*, 14, *14*, *112*, *114*, 120, *123*, 124, *124*, *125*, 128, *129*, 130–3, *130*
Anne, Queen, 182
Appelton House, Sandringham, 67
Arden family, 193–7, *195*, 198
Argyll, 9th Duke of, 24, 41, 182
Armstrong-Jones, Lady Sarah, *11*, 98, 110, *110*, *111*, *119*, 135, 137, *137*, 150, 159
Artaxias I, 183
Arthur, Prince, Duke of Connaught, *18*, *19*, 24, 34, *34–5*, 36, 38, *38*, 39, 99
Arthur of Connaught, Prince, *see* Connaught, Prince Arthur of
Arundel, Earl of, 188
Ashdown, Dulcie M., 200
Ashton, Sir George, 200
Astor, Nancy Lady, 189
Athlone, Earl of, 24, 40, 81, *123*

B

Babington-Smith, Susan, 132
Balmoral Castle, 9, 85, 110, *114*, *130*, *135*, 169, 170, *170*
Barnes, Mrs, *122*, 123
Barnwell Manor, Peterborough, 156, *157*, 159
Barrington, Lady Caroline, 34, 188
Barton, Anthony, 110
Battenberg, Prince Alexander of, *22*, 24
Battenberg, Princess Alice of, *16*, 24, 39, 130, 180, 190, 198
Battenberg, Princess Ena of, *22*, 24
Battenberg, Prince Henry of, *16*, 24, 41, 182
Battenberg, Princess Henry of, *see* Beatrice, Princess
Battenberg, Prince Leopold of, *22*, 24
Battenberg, Prince Louis of, 24, 41, *57*, 190
Battenberg, Princess Louis of, *see* Victoria of Hesse, Princess
Battenberg, Prince Maurice of, *22*, 24
Battiscombe, Georgina, 64, 200
Beatrice, Princess, *16*, *22*, 24, 34, 36–7, *39*, 41, 53, 78, 182
Bedales School, 110, *111*
Bellaigues, Vicomtesse de, 104
Bill, Mrs ("Lalla"), 82, *82*, 86, 88, 157

Birch, Henry, 33
Birkhall, Balmoral, 148
Black Prince, the, 182
Blackburn, Mrs Mary, 59
Bogart, Humphrey, 180, 189
Bolton, Anne, 169
Bowes-Lyon, Hon David, 108, *111*, 122, *123*, 183
Bowes-Lyon, Lady Elizabeth, *see* Elizabeth, Queen, the Queen Mother
Bowes-Lyon, Hon Fiona, 150
Brabourne, Lady, 123, *123*
Bracebridge, Richard, 193
Brown, Dr, 53
Brown, Richard, 126
Bricka, Mlle, 84, 85–6
Bridgeman, Marigold, 110
Buccleuch, Duke of, 159
Buckingham Palace, *11*, 12, 27, 106, *116*, *119*, 121, 125, 134, 149, 154
Burghersh, Maud, 197
Burghley, William Cecil, Lord, 186
Butter, Mrs David, 150

C

Camberwell School of Art, *111*
Cambridge, Duchess of, 24, 61, 62, 190
Cambridge, Lady May, 103
Canute, King, 184, 185
Campbell, Judith, 200
Canning, Lady, 33
Carew, Sir George, 186
Cathcart, Helen, 200
Catherine the Great, of Russia, 185
Cavendish, Lady Elizabeth, 110
Chapel Royal, *see* St James's Palace
Charles I, 108, 184
Charles II, 184
Charles V, 183
Charles VI, 183
Charles, Prince of Wales, 6, 9, *9*, *11*, 12, *12–13*, 14, *112*, *115–16*, 120, 121–5, *123*, *124*, 125–6, 126–30, *126–30*, *132*, *135*, 151, 159, *170*, *178*, 180, 182, 184–6, 190, 197, 198
Charles of Denmark, Prince, *see* Haakon VII, King of Norway
Charles Edward, Prince, 24, 39
Charlotte of Prussia, Princess, *41*, 190
Charrier, Mlle, 30
Chaucer, Geoffrey, 197
Cheam School, 129
Chiswick House, 62, *63*
Christian I, King of Denmark, 180, 185

Christian IX, King of Denmark, 52, 180, 190
Christian of Schleswig-Holstein, Prince, 40
Churchill, Arabella, 184
Churchill, Randolph, 9
Churchill, Sir Winston, 188, 193
Chuter-Ede, James, 121
Clarence, Duke of, *see* Albert Victor, Prince
Clarence House, 12, 91, 110, 123, *123*
Clark, Sir James, 26, 36
Clear, Celia, 200
Coggan, Dr Donald, 133
Collins, Mr, 61
Colman, Lady Mary, 167
Connaught, Arthur, Duke of, *see* Arthur, Prince
Connaught, Arthur, Prince of, 22, 24, 50
Connaught, Duchess of, *22*, 24
Connaught, Margaret, Princess of 22, 24
Connaught, Patricia, Princess of, 22, 24, 121
Constantine, King of the Hellenes, 46, 154
Coppins, Iver, 66, 146, *146*, 149, *149*
Corti, Egon Caesar, Conte, 200
Crawford, Marion, 104, *104*, 105, 109, 120
Crawley, Canon, 105

D

Dalton, Rev John Neale, 62–3
Darnley, Henry, Earl of, 184
Dartmouth, Raine, Countess of, 169
Davidson, Sir Arthur, 65
De Stoeckl, Agnes, Baroness, 146, 200
Derby, Earl of, 9, 183
Devonshire, Duke of, 62, 180, 186
Diana, Princess of Wales, 8, *11*, 14, *14*, 120, 166–70, *167–70*, *178*, 183–4, 190, 193, 197
Donaldson, Frances, 200
Dracul, Vlad, 184
Duff, David, 200
Dussau, Mlle José, 87

E

Edward III, 183, 185, 193
Edward IV, 182, 185, 188
Edward VII, 6, 9, *18*, 24, 29, *29*, 32, 38, 42, 50–67, *53*, *74*, 79, 81, 84, 89, 180, 182, 190
Edward VIII, Duke of Windsor, 22, 48, 68, 72–4, 76, 79, 80, *80–1*, 84, 86, *86*, 87, 90–1, 98, 108, 200
Edward, Prince, *11*, 14, *114–15*, *119*,

120, 133, *134*, 136–7, *137*, 150, 159
Edward George, Prince, Duke of Kent, *11*, 14, 144, 145–8, *145*, *146*, 166
Elizabeth I, 186
Elizabeth II, 6, 8–9, *11*, *12*, *12*, 13, 89–90, 91, *91*, *93*, *94*, 97, 98, *98*, 99–110, *112*, *119*, 120–9, *123*, *130*, 166, 180, 190, 198
Elizabeth, Queen, the Queen Mother, 8, *11*, *12*, 14, 76, 90, *91*, *93*, 97, 98–106, *100*, *111*, *116*, 123, 130, 156, 166, 180, 183, 187, 190, 198
Elizabeth, Queen of Bohemia, 182
Elizabeth of Hesse, Princess, *20*
Elphinstone, Lady, 99
Elphinstone, Major, *38*
Elphinstone, Hon Andrew, 130
Ena of Battenberg, Princess, *see* Battenberg, Princess Ena of
Ernest, King of Hanover, 27, 39
Ernest, Prince, *20*
Essex, Robert Devereux, Earl of, 186
Eton College, 148–51, 158
Eton End School, Datchet, 150–1

F

Fellowes, Laura Jane, 169
Fellowes, Robert, 169
Fenton, Roger, *18*, *20*, *32*
Fermoy, Hon Frances, *see* Shand Kydd, Hon Mrs
Fermoy, Maurice, 4th Lord, 166, 180, 188, *189*, 190
Fermoy, Ruth, Lady, 166, 188, 190
Fife, Duke of, 50, 64–5, 182
Finch, Frederick, 86
Fleming, Bishop Lancelot, 159
Floyd, John, 167
Fox, Miss, 148
Fox, Mrs William, 167
Frankland, Noble, 200
Frederick William of Prussia, Prince (later Kaiser Frederick III), 24, 36, 38
Frogmore House, Windsor, 52–3, 80, 85
Fuller, Charles, 53

G

Gatcombe Park, *9*, *13*, 133
Geddes, Mrs Andrew, 154
Geelong Grammar School, 130
George I, King of Greece, *46*, 52, 156, 180, 190

George III, 24, 180, 182, 187
George IV, 29
George V, 6, 9, *22*, 24, 39, *42*, 46, 50, 53–4, *54–5*, 59–60, 61, 63–6, 68, 71, 76–90, *79*, 89, 99–100, 166, 180, 190
George VI, 12, *22*, 48, 68, *72–4*, 76, 81, *82*, 83, *83–4*, 86–7, *87*, 90–1, *91*, 97, 98, 98–106, *116*, 121–2, *123*, 125, 156, 166, 180, 183, 190, 198
George, Prince, Duke of Kent, 48, 68, 76, 81, *81–2*, *84*, 88, 91, 97, 103, 120, 144, 145–6, *146*, 148, 182
George of Greece, Prince, *46*, 123
George of Hanover, Princess, 137
Ghengis Khan, 184
Gibbs, Frederick, *20*, 33, *33*
Gibbs School, Kensington, 137, *137*, 151
Gibson, Charles Dana, 189
Gilmour, Alexander, 167
Glamis Castle, 108, *108*, *111*
Gloucester, Duchess of (Princess Mary), 33
Gloucester, Duchess of (Lady Alice Montagu-Douglas-Scott), *see* Alice, Princess, Duchess of Gloucester
Gloucester, Duchess of (Birgitte van Deurs), *14*, 144, *158*, 159
Gloucester, Henry, Duke of, *see* Henry, Prince, Duke of Gloucester
Gloucester, William, Duke of, *see* William of Gloucester, Prince
Glyndwr, Owain, 180, 185
Goodhart, Joseph, 150
Gordonstoun School, 130, 136–7, *150*, 151
Gore, John, 66, 78, 200
Gort, Viscount, 156
Gower, Lord Ronald, 51
Grafton, Duke of, 184
Granville, Countess, 108, 122
Greville, Charles, 25
Grey, Lady Jane, 180, 186
Grey of Powis, Lord, 185
Grigg, John, 6
Guérin, Mlle Georgina, 104

H

Haakon VII, King of Norway, 50, 67, 122, 156
Halliday, F. E., 200
Hambro, Clementine, 170
Hamilton, Caroline, 132
Hamilton, Lady Cynthia, *see* Spencer, Cynthia, Countess of
Hampden family, 193, 198
Hansell, Henry Peter, 86, 87

Harewood, 6th Earl of, see Lascelles,
   Viscount
Harold Godwinson, King, 185
Harrison, Michael, 63, 200
Hawkins, Lady Margaret, 156
Hay, Sir Philip, 150
Hayter, Sir George, 25
Heatherdown School, 136–7, 150–1
Heathfield School, 148
Helen of Waldeck, Princess, 156
Helena, Princess, 24, 63–4
Henry I, 184
Henry IV, 182, 185
Henry V, 185
Henry VII, 180, 185, 193, 197
Henry VIII, 182, 185, 186
Henry, Prince, Duke of Gloucester, 14, 48,
   68, 74, 76, 81, 82, 84, 87–8, 91, 144,
   154, 154
Henry of Battenberg, Prince, see Battenberg,
   Prince Henry of
Henry of Battenberg, Princess, see
   Beatrice, Princess
Henry of Prussia, Prince, 41
Herbert, Lord, Earl of Pembroke, 150
Highgrove House, 189
Hildyard, Sarah, 33
Hill House School, 127, 129
Holden, Anthony, 200
Holstein, Duchy of, 52
Honeycombe, Gordon, 200
Hua, Gabriel, 87
Hull, Mrs, 34
Hyde, Anne, 182

I

Ingrid, Princess, of Sweden, 108
Institut Alpin Videmanette, 169
Irene, Princess, 20

J

James I, 180, 183
James II, 182, 184
John of Wales, Prince, 50, 58–9
John of York, Prince, 68, 76, 81, 88

K

Kelly, Sgt, 126
Kensington Palace, 149
Keppel, Lavinia, 137

Kent, Duchess of, see Marina, Princess;
   Worsley, Katharine
Kent, Edward, Duke of, see Edward George,
   Prince
Kent, George, Duke of, see George, Prince,
   Duke of Kent
Kimball, Sophie, 169
King, Stella, 200
Knight, Clara ("Alla"), 100, 101, 103, 106
Knollys, Sir William, 57

L

Lacey, Robert, 200
Lafontaine, Dr Leopold, 184
Laird, Dorothy, 200
Laking, Sir Francis, 86, 87, 88
Landseer, Sir Edwin, 30, 31
Lang, Cosmo, Archbishop of Canterbury,
   97, 108
Lascelles, Viscount, 6th Earl of Harewood,
   64, 76, 91, 121, 122
Lehzen, Baroness, 25, 29
Leicester, Robert Dudley, Earl of, 186, 196
Leo XII, Pope, 64
Leopold, King of the Belgians, 29, 30
Leopold, Prince, Duke of Albany, 18, 24,
   36, 36, 38–9, 39
Leopold of Battenberg, Prince, see
   Battenberg, Prince Leopold of
Leslie, C. R., 27
Lichfield, Countess of, 133
Lichfield, Earl of, 11
Lightbody, Helen, 122, 124, 126, 128,
   129, 156
Lilly, Mrs, 27, 32
Linley, Viscount, 11, 98, 110, 110, 111,
   119, 136–7
Llewellyn the Great, 185
Locock, Dr, 26–7
Longford, Elizabeth, Countess of, 200
Lorne, Marquess of, see Argyll, 9th Duke of
Louis of Battenberg, Prince, see Battenberg,
   Prince Louis of
Louis of Battenberg, Princess, see Victoria
   of Hesse, Princess
Louis IV, Grand Duke of Hesse-Darmstadt,
   20, 24, 37, 190
Louis of Hesse, Prince, 137
Louise, Queen of Denmark, 46, 56
Louise, Princess, Duchess of Argyll, 18, 24,
   33–4, 39, 41, 41, 54, 182
Louise, Princess Royal, Duchess of Fife, 39,
   46, 50, 56, 56, 59–60, 62, 64–5, 77,
   91, 182

Louise of Prussia, Princess, 24, 39
Ludgrove School, 148
Lumley, Lady Serena, 148
Lyon, Sir John, 184
Lyttelton, Lady, 30, 32, 34, 188

M

Macclesfield, Lady, 53, 56
Macdonald, Margaret ("Bobo"), 100, 106
Macdonald, Ruby, 100
Magdalene College, Cambridge, 158
Magnus, Sir Philip, 58, 200
Margaret, Princess, 8, *8, 11*, 12, 14, *89, 93, 94*, 98, 100, *100–107*, 106, 108–10, *110*, 123, *123*, 150
Margaret of Connaught, *see* Connaught, Margaret, Princess of
Margaret of Scotland, Princess, 180, 182
Margarita of Hohenlöhe-Langenburg, Princess, 130
Marie, Princess, of Edinburgh, 76, *76*
Marie, Grand Duchess, of Russia, 38
Marie of Greece, Princess, *46*
Marie Feodorovna, Tsarina, 52, 54
Marie Louise, Princess, *22*, 24, 41, 157
Marina, Princess, 76, 91, 103, 120, 144, 145, *146*, 148–9, 182
Marlborough House, 52, 53, 57, *57*, 62, 84, 125
Marples, Morris, 200
Marlborough, Sarah, Duchess of, 188
Marten, Sir Henry, 104, 109
Mary, Princess Royal, *22*, 48, *64*, 68, 73–4, 76, 81, *82*, 84, 86, *86*, 91, 98–9
Mary, Queen, 9, *22*, 24, 50, 62, *62*, 64–5, *68, 71*, 76–91, *89, 90*, 99, 103, *123*, 125, 146, 149, 157, 182, 184, 190
Mary, Queen of Scots, 180, 183, 184
Matson, John, 200
Maud, Princess, of Fife, *48*
Maud of Wales, Princess, *46*, 50, 58, *59–60*, 61, *62*, 67, *71*
Maurice of Battenberg, Prince, *see* Battenberg, Prince Maurice of
May, Princess, *20*
May of Teck, Princess, *see* Mary, Queen
McCorquodale, Neil, 169
McPherson, Mary, 149, 151
Mecklenburg-Strelitz, Augusta, Grand Duchess of, 24, 64, 190
Melbourne, Lord, 26
Michael of Kent, Prince, *11*, 14, *14*, 144, 146–8, 154, *154*
Michael of Kent, Princess, 14, *14*, 144, *153*

Milford Haven, Dowager Marchioness of, 123, *123*
Millin, Sarah Gertrude, 108
Moncreiffe of that Ilk, Sir Iain, 184
Montagu-Douglas-Scott, Lady Alice, *see* Alice, Princess, Duchess of Gloucester
Mordaunt, Sir Charles, 58
Morgan, J. Pierpont, Jr, 189
Morrah, Dermot, 129, 200
Moss, Pat, 133
Mountbatten of Burma, Earl, 24, *57*, 120, 128, 130, 182

N

Napoleon III, 57
Nether Lypiatt Manor, Stroud, 154
Nevill, Lord Rupert, 110
Nicholas I, Tsar, 185
Nicholas III, Tsar, 24
Nicholas of Greece, Prince, 145
Nicolson, Sir Harold, 200
Northumberland, John Dudley, Duke of, 186

O

Ogilvy, Hon Angus, *11*, *108*, 136, 144, 149–52, *152*
Ogilvy, James Robert, *11*, *115*, 137, 144, 150–2, *152*, 154
Ogilvy, Marina Victoria, *11*, *115*, *119*, 144, 151–2, *152*, 154
Olav V, King of Norway, 50, 67
Olga, Queen of Greece, *46*
Osborne House, 9, *22*, 85, *85*; Swiss Cottage, 36, *37*

P

Packer, Mrs, 34
Paget, Gerald, 182
Paget, Sir James, 56
Palmerston, Lord, 25
Park House, Sandringham, 166, *167*, 168
Parker, Lt Commander Michael, 121
Parker-Bowles, Lt-Col Andrew, 133
Parnell, Judith, 167
Patricia of Connaught, Princess, *see* Connaught, Princess Patricia of
Peebles, Catherine, 128, *129*, 136–7, 148
Pelly, Claire, 150
Pembroke, Earl of, *see* Herbert, Lord, Earl of Pembroke

Pembroke, Mary, Countess of, 186
Penn, Mrs Eric, 110
Philip, Prince, Duke of Edinburgh, 6, 9, 11, 12, 24, 57, 98, 112, 119, 120–8, 123, 148, 180, 182, 190, 198
Phillips, Captain Mark, 14, 120, 130, 133
Phillips, Peter, 6, 9, 13, 120, 130, 133, 133–4
Phillips, Zara, 6, 120, 133
Phipps, Rev Simon, 110
Pinker, George, 133, 159
Pitman, Virginia, 169
Plunket, Lord, 110
Ponsonby, Sir Frederick, 63, 77, 200
Pope-Hennessy, James, 76, 200
Pratt, Mrs Michael, 167
Pride, Carolyn, 169

R

Raleigh, Joan, 197
Ramsay, Lady Patricia, see Connaught, Princess Patricia of
Rattle, Olive, 151–2
Ratsey, Mrs, 34
Reibnitz, Baroness Marie-Christine von, see Michael of Kent, Princess
Rhédey, Count Lazzlo, 183
Richard of Gloucester, Prince, 137, 144, 156, 157, 157
Riddlesworth, Hall, Thetford, 168
Ridsdale, Elizabeth, 168
Robert, Cedric Lane, 156
Roch, Castle, 189
Roche family, 180, 188–9, 190, 198
Rockefeller, Nelson, 189
Roosevelt, F. D., 146
Rosebery, Lord, 65
Rosslyn, Earl of, 64
Round, Dr Horace, 188
Rowcliffe, Jean, 154
Rowe, Helen, 121, 135
Rowse, A. L., 200
Royal Lodge, Windsor, 102, 128
Rudge, Ruth, 168

S

Salisbury, Lord, 64, 186
Sandringham House, 6, 52, 52, 59, 62, 77, 80, 82, 85, 89, 90, 131, 134, 166, 167
Sarsfield, Mary, 184
Schwarzenburg, Prince Karl Johannes von, 154

Scott, Lord William, 156
Scott-Giles, C.W., 197, 200
Shakerley, Lady Elizabeth, 154
Shakespeare, William, 187, 192–7, 198
Shand Kydd, Hon Mrs, 166–7, 188, 190
Shand Kydd, Peter, 167
Sheen Lodge, 65, 77
Silfield School, King's Lynn, 168
Simpson, Mrs Wallis (Duchess of Windsor), 76, 90
Sinclair, David, 200
Smith, Captain Henry Abel, see Abel Smith, Captain Henry
Snowdon, Earl of, 9, 11, 98, 109, 110, 111, 137
Snowman, Dr Jacob, 123
Somerset, Edward Seymour, Duke of, 180, 186
Somerset, Lady Geraldine, 54, 61
Southey, Mrs, 30
Spencer family, 187, 187–9
Spencer, 7th Earl, 166, 168, 184, 186, 188, 190, 198
Spencer, 8th Earl, 166, 166, 190, 198
Spencer, Lord Charles (Viscount Althorp), 166
Spencer, Cynthia, Countess, 166, 184
Spencer, Lady Diana, see Diana, Princess of Wales
Spencer, Lady Jane, 166, 169
Spencer, Lady Sarah, 166, 169
St Andrews, Earl of, 11, 119, 144, 149, 149, 150, 154, 154
St Aubyn, Giles, 148, 158, 200
St Clair-Erskine, Lady Sybil, 64
St George's Chapel, Windsor, 29, 50
St James's Palace, 37; Chapel Royal, 25, 28, 77, 154
St Mary's School, Wantage, 151–2
St Paul's Preparatory School, 151
St Peter's Court School, 88
Stanislaus II, 184
Stephen, King, 185
Stevens, Mrs Jane, 110
Stewart, Mrs Jackie, 133
Stockmar, Baron, 30, 32–3
Strathmore and Kinghorne, Earl of, 99, 180, 183, 184, 189, 190, 198
Suffolk, Charles Brandon, Duke of, 180, 185
Sumner, Miss, 110
Sunningdale Preparatory School, 149
Sussex House School, 151

T

Teck, May, Duchess of, 24, 61–2, 62, 64, 67, 190
Teck, Francis, Duke of, 24, 62, 190
Teck, Princess May of, see Mary, Queen
Thatched House Lodge, Richmond, 151, 152
Thomas, Hugh, 133
Throckmorton, Robert, 194
Thurston, Mrs, 34
Tisdall, E. E. P., 200
Trinity College, Cambridge, 130

U

Ulster, Earl of, 144, 159

V

Vickers, Hugo, 200
Victoria, Queen, 6, 8–9, 13, 16–41, 22, 25, 27, 35, 39, 41, 51–3, 64, 77–8, 79–80, 84, 180, 182, 183, 190
Victoria of Hesse, Princess, 16, 20, 24, 40–1, 57, 180, 190
Victoria of Schleswig-Holstein, Princess, 22
Victoria of Wales, Princess, 46, 50, 57, 59–60, 61, 62, 65–6, 71, 108
Victoria Adelaide, Princess Royal, 6, 13, 18, 24, 26, 27, 28, 30–2, 38
Villiers, Barbara, 184
von Hauke, Countess Julia, 184, 190
von Hauke, Count Maurice, 184, 190

W

Wagner, Sir Anthony, 183, 200
Waldegrave, Henrietta, Lady, 184
Wallace, Edgar, 91
Walsingham, Sir Francis, 186
Walter, Lucy, 184
Ward, Edith, 88
Warwick, Earls of, 193, 196, 197
Washington family, 180, 186, 187, 187, 193
Wellesley House, Broadstairs, 158
Wellington, Duke of, 34, 35
Wentworth Day, J., 200
West Heath School, Sevenoaks, 168
Westmorland, Earl of, 110
Whalesborough, Sir John, 197, 198

Wheeler-Bennett, Sir John W., 200
Whippingham, 41, 63
White Lodge, Richmond, 78–80, 99
Wilkinson, Christine, 159
William I, 185
William II, Kaiser, 24, 38, 41
William IV, 25
William of Gloucester, Prince, 144, 154, 156, 157, 158
Windisch-Graetz, Prince Hugo, 154
Windlesham Moor, Berkshire, 122, 123
Windsor, Duchess of, see Simpson, Mrs Wallis
Windsor, Duke of, see Edward VIII
Windsor, House of, 6
Windsor, Lord Alexander, see Ulster, Earl of
Windsor, Lady Davina, 144, 158, 159
Windsor, Lord Frederick, 144, 153, 154
Windsor, Lady Gabriella ("Ella"), 144, 152, 153, 154
Windsor, Lady Helen, 11, 137, 144, 150, 150
Windsor, Lord Nicholas, 11, 144, 151, 151
Windsor, Lady Rose, 144, 159
Windsor Castle, 32, 32, 41, 105
Winterhalter, Franz, 6, 29, 34, 35
Wood Farm, Wolferton, 88
Woodham-Smith, Cecil, 200
Woods, Very Rev Robert, 150
Woodville, Elizabeth, 185
Work family, 180, 188–9, 190
Worsley, Katharine, Duchess of Kent, 11, 14, 137, 144, 149
Worsley, Oliver, 149

Y

York Cottage, Sandringham, 77, 81–2, 86, 89
York House, 158
Young England Kindergarten, 170

Acknowledgements

Numerals refer to page numbers (abbreviations: T. top; B. bottom; C. centre; R. right; L. left).

Grateful acknowledgement is made to H.M. Queen Elizabeth II for her gracious permission to reproduce the paintings from the Royal Collection on pages 7, 31 and 35, and the photographs from the Royal Archives, Windsor, on pages 18, 19, 20, 21, 32B, 33, 34, 36, 37, 38, 39, 40L, 40C, 41B, 44, 46–7, 55, 56, 57R, 60, 62T, 66, 67L, 72B, 73T, 76, 82L, 83, 84, 85, 87, 93, 95, 98 and 108; and to the following:
BBC Hulton Pictire Library 12B, 13B, 17, 29, 40R, 48, 49, 51, 53, 67R, 69, 70–71, 72T, 75, 79, 80, 81, 86, 99, 102, 104, 105, 106, 109, 121, 122, 123B, 126, 128, 129, 144;
Janet and Colin Bord 189;
Camera Press/Cecil Beaton 147, 152;
Camera Press/Tom Blau 157L;
Camera Press/Patrick Lichfield 10B, 114, 135;
Camera Press/Snowdon 9B, 111L, 133, 137R, 140–41;
College of Arms, by courtesy of the Garter King 2, 179;
Colour Library International 123T;
Reginald Davis 6, 10TR, 115TL, 119, 127, 134R, 143;
Tim Graham 14, 15L, 15CR, 15BR, 131CR, 131BR, 164, 165, 166, 167L, 171L, 187;
Anwar Hussein 10TL, 15TR, 52, 115B, 131L, 131TR, 163, 170, 171TR, 171CR;
Illustrated London News 8, 9T, 12T, 25, 26, 32T, 54, 89, 90, 94, 101R;
Nigel O'Gorman 41T;
Photographers International 15, 136, 138, 142, 169, 171BR;
Popperfoto 13T, 22–3, 27, 43, 45, 57L, 59, 62B, 63, 64, 73B, 74, 77, 82R, 96, 97, 100T, 101L, 101R, 103, 107, 110, 113, 115TR, 116, 117, 124, 130, 132, 134L, 137L, 145, 149, 150, 151, 153, 155, 156, 157R, 158;
Press Association 167R, 168;
Syndication International 11, 118, 139, 162;
John Topham Picture Library 91, 100B, 111R, 125, 152, 157L.